Bloomsbury Methuen Drama
An imprint of Bloomsbury Publishing Plc

B L O O M S B U R Y

LONDON • OXFORD • NEW YORK • NEW DELHI • SYDNEY

Bloomsbury Methuen Drama

An imprint of Bloomsbury Publishing Plc

Imprint previously known as Methuen Drama

50 Bedford Square	1385 Broadway
London	New York
WC1B 3DP, UK	NY 10018, USA

www.bloomsbury.com

**BLOOMSBURY, METHUEN DRAMA and the Diana logo
are trademarks of Bloomsbury Publishing Plc**

First published 2017

© Roy Williams, 2017

British Library Cataloguing-in-Publication Data
A catalogue record for this book is available from the British Library.

ISBN: PB: 978-1-3500-6544-4
ePDF: 978-1-3500-6545-1
eBook: 978-1-3500-6546-8

Library of Congress Cataloging-in-Publication Data
A catalog record for this book is available from the Library of Congress.

Series: Modern Plays

Cover design: Olivia D'Cruz
Cover image © iStock/alejandrophotography

Typeset by Country Setting, Kingsdown, Kent CT14 8ES
Printed and bound in Great Britain

To find out more about our authors and books visit www.bloomsbury.com.
Here you will find extracts, author interviews, details of forthcoming events
and the option to sign up for our newsletters.

Dedicated to

Terry Sue-Patt
(1964–2015)

and

Mark Farmer
(1962–2016)

The power of your actions
helped to change my life.
RW

The Firm

For Lincoln Hudson, my brother

The Firm was first presented at Hampstead Theatre on
27 October 2017, with the following cast and creative team:

Trent   Delroy Atkinson
Gus   Clinton Blake
Fraser   Simon Coombs
Leslie   Jay Simpson
Selwyn   Clarence Smith

Director   Denis Lawson
Designer   Alex Marker
Lighting   Neill Brinkworth
Sound   John Leonard

My deepest thanks to the Barnfield boys: Godwin Nwaokobia,
Julius Francis, Michael Hearn and Steve Macaulay, for your
friendship, your trust and for telling me so many brilliant
stories.

Characters

Leslie, *white, late forties / early fifties*
Gus, *black, late forties / early fifties*
Trent, *black, late forties / early fifties*
Selwyn, *black, late forties / early fifties*
Fraser, *mixed race, twenties*

Setting

A renovated pub in South London. Present day.

The play opens in an expensive-looking refurbished pub. Comfy-looking leather seats. The bar would look at home in a fifties American diner. Clean tile floors. Cream-coloured walls. There are several bottles of expensive champagne and champagne glasses on the bar.

An old-fashioned fifties-style Wurlitzer jukebox, looking quite pristine and brand new rests in the corner.

Leslie *and* **Gus** *are onstage.* **Leslie** *is standing on a chair, putting up a 'Welcome home Sean' decoration on the wall.*

Leslie   . . . Anyhow two, twos, as soon as me and Selwyn got nicked yeah, on remand we was, no messing, no question. After they are done processing us in the nick, they are marching us through reception on our way to the wings, when they have to stop and deal with some incident that's been going on. They sit us down in an office, warning us not to move an inch or even breathe. Have I not told you this?

Gus   Well, you're telling me now.

Leslie   For only about thirty seconds yeah, they have their backs to us, can't see us or what we are about. Selwyn is going all telepathic, telling me with his face to have a gander to my right, over by the desk. As I live, Gus, there is an open safe and straight off my eyeballs were going all Roger Rabbit. No one knows about the sight of corn better than me, right or wrong?

Gus   Oh, I know, you thieving little cunt.

Leslie   I could tell, within seconds, there was about five hundred quid in there. Must of have been petty cash or summin. Without skipping a beat, I swear to you, I leap over the desk, swipe the notes out from that safe, stuff them down my pants, and back in my seat, like the Flash!

Gus   Fuck off!

Leslie   Three seconds to spare –

Gus   Move!

Leslie   – before the screws turned around again, without a clue to what happened, not a whiff! If I lie, I die. Am I good?

Gus   You're a legend, Leslie. It's always been said.

Leslie   Selwyn as well.

Gus   How come they didn't search you?

Leslie   Search for what? They already had us stripped bare, we were on our way to the wings with our bags, weren't you listening? Two days later, we're ghosted out. Case dismissed. According to my brief, the CPS fucked it right up for themselves, crucial evidence gone missing or summin. So, on my way out, this screw grabs my neck, holds me up against the door, going, 'It was you, yer cunt, weren't it, weren't it?' 'Weren't what?' I ask. He goes, 'I don't know for the life of me how, but it was you who swiped that money, weren't it, in less than twenty seconds? Who the fuck are you, Houdini's long lost boy?' I goes, 'Nuh, nuh, don't be silly.'

Gus   You had that money all that time you were inside?

Leslie   I fucking walked out of the nick with it. As soon as we were on the out, I treated me and Sel to a proper full English.

Gus   I'm scared to ask this, where'd you hide it, the money?

Leslie   Kept it on me, down my pants.

Gus   You had a monkey up yer arse?

Leslie   No, not up my arse, down my pants.

Gus   24/7?

Leslie   Who's ever gonna think I have five hundred boys on me in there?

Gus   Yer a legend, mate.

Leslie   Gotta give it up for Sel, though.

Gus   Why? You did the graft. It's your tickle.

Leslie   Cos he eyeballed it in the first place, he put me on it. Him and his eagle eyes are legendary all over South, Gus, for a paper shout, you know that.

Gus   Is this your way of saying, you are not going to have a word with him for me?

Leslie   I did have a word.

Gus   Well, what was it that you said to him?

Leslie   What it was you told me to say to him.

Gus   Which was what, Les?

Leslie   That your answer is no.

Gus   Well that does not seem to be working.

Leslie   Well, I'm sorry about that.

Gus   I can't be dealing with his shit, Les.

Leslie   What do you want me to do, what do you want me to say?

Gus   Higher.

Leslie *moves the sign higher.*

Leslie   I don't know why you are getting so wet about it. You know Selwyn already, man.

Gus   That is why I asked you to talk to him. One phone call, mi mek, just one, to bring the boys back together, and he's on my arse wid it, non-stop.

Leslie   You should let him roll with it, like I do. Let him chat his shit, get it out of his system and that. So he thinks he is still the big man. Then you blow him off. Did he tell you who it was?

Gus   Some younger. I mean, who robs a supermarket nowadays? Answer me that, it doesn't mek sense.

It's dropping down.

Leslie *adjusts the sign.*

Gus   Higher, mate, come on.

Leslie   It's fine as it is.

Gus   Alright, but you know how Shaun feels about his name?

Leslie   By the time them gals we got for him are done, the last thing he will be worrying about is his name.

Gus   Just as long as they ain't some ugly-ass bitches.

Leslie   Trust me, blud.

Gus   *Blud?* Did you just say *blud* to me? Where did that come from?

Leslie   Nowhere.

Gus   Just do me a favour. At some point tonight just take Selwyn aside. Tell him I said no, and that he needs to have a word with himself. And while yer at it, make sure that he takes his pills.

Leslie   I was planning on having a good time tonight, I'm not Selwyn's babysitter. Leave him alone if he wants to carry on wid his hype.

Gus   I don't want him giving me the arsehole and go flaring up like he does.

Leslie   He just wants to feel we are still the firm.

Gus   We are still the firm.

Leslie   Of course we are.

Gus   But?

Leslie   There is no but.

Gus   Bollocks.

Leslie   Bollocks yourself. We ain't had a session in years.

Gus   And whose fault is that?

Leslie   How's Naomi doing?

Gus   Naomi?

Leslie   Her new school and that.

Gus   Oh, Leslie, that was a classy segue.

Leslie   Step off.

Gus   Just praising yer, cha rass. Full of subtext and shit.

Leslie   Call it what you like, am just asking after my goddaughter, that is all.

Gus   She's sweet, least she will be.

Leslie   Will be?

Gus   I had Andrea giving me the arsehole the other night. Turns out, Naomi has been calling her every day, crying about how she hates her new school and that she wants come home.

Leslie   She's thirteen, mate.

Gus   She's a thirteen-year-old with a forty grand a year education who needs to sort her shit out. I gave her a bell myself, I goes, 'Naomi, run away if you feel but don't even think about bringing yourself home, I don't business at all if yer thirteen. You'll be a thirteen-year-old uneducated bitch gal wid no home, so tek yer arse back to that school and hit the books.'

Leslie   You really said that, you said 'bitch' to yer own daughter?

Gus   Damn right, I said that. Except the bitch part. Forty grand a year though, Les, I mean, have a word!

Leslie   That's a lot of cheddar.

Gus   My cheddar. I do what I want with it.

Leslie   Yes, you most certainly do, mate.

Gus   I saw Sam Hardy's little sister the other day. Sharon.

Leslie   And?

Gus   She was saying Sam took another turn. They can't cope with him any more, they're gonna put him in a nursing home. Shame that.

Leslie   Now, *that's* a segue. Little bit over the top, but a segue nonetheless, eh, Gus?

Gus   Anyhow, I funded Sharon a couple of grand, on behalf of us, the boys and that. The guy's a cabbage now. I thought it was the least we could do.

Leslie   You're a proper hero, Gus.

Gus   She seemed happy.

Still don't look straight enough.

Leslie   Well, I'm done with it.

Gus *pours* **Leslie** *a glass of champagne.*

Gus   Salut!

Leslie   Salut!

They clink their glasses.

Gus   Twelve years, Les.

Leslie   Long time.

Gus   Motherfuck! Now we gotta be sure?

Leslie   About?

Gus   We don't go all emotional and that. We don't cuddle up to him, none of that shit.

Leslie   Did you say cuddle?

Gus   No huggy-kissy from anyone. Let's be men about it.

Leslie   I ain't kissing Shaun. I never thought about kissing him.

Gus   I know you ain't.

Leslie   Right.

Gus   Am just saying, let's rein it in.

Leslie   Is there a reason why you are telling me this?

Gus   I don't want anyone getting carried away.

Leslie   You mean you don't want me getting carried away, don't yer? What the fuck, Gus?

Gus   Ease up, yeah?

Leslie   You ease up, cunt.

Gus   Down, boy, calm.

Leslie   I am calm. I am calm as I can be with calm. It's about her, isn't it?

Gus   No, it isn't. Claire is a sort, a raving, lawd knows what she sees in you, but there you go. Them's the breaks. I look forward to meeting her one day.

Leslie   Who's Claire?

Gus   You don't know the name of your own woman, Les?

Leslie   Her name is Jan.

Gus   It's what I said.

Leslie   You said Claire.

Gus   Never again Jan! Got it.

Leslie   Never mind yourself about me. You want to find yourself a woman, quick time. You and Andrea broke up how long, three years?

Gus   Two years.

Leslie   She's moved on, time you did.

Gus   Point taken.

Leslie   Giving me shit.

Gus   Are you done? Seriously? I rank you, Les, you know that.

Leslie   I didn't plan to move in on it. She's my probation officer, Gus. Two twos, when I met her, I took one look, and say, Jesuuuss, wat de rah! What I wouldn't give to fling dat down sometime! Just my type an all. Kim Wilde lookalike, before the flab.

Gus   Kim Wilde?

Leslie   The singer, Gus.

Gus   This trout of yours is a white chick?

Leslie   Yeah.

Gus   You change sides?

Leslie   I never changed sides.

Gus   Nobody love de black pum more than you, Leslie.

Leslie   I love all pum. I'm the United Nations on all things to do wid de pum. Point is, grinding your probation officer, regardless of the colour of de pum my friend is a big no-no!

Gus   Don't do it then.

Leslie   You mad or what? Jan had it all going on for herself, tight blue jeans and a blouse that hug de body. You know what she did for me on our first date?

Gus (*excited*)   Oh, yes?

Leslie   Made me a cup of tea.

Gus   What?

Leslie   Not your regular PG Tips and that, herbal or something, and it was proper nice! Take out the teabag, a teaspoon of honey, and that'll work! *You get me?* Then she stroked my face all good, rubbed my shoulders, proper nice.

Oh lawd! She knows right where to go, every time! What? Why are you looking at me like that?

Gus   'You get me?'

Leslie   What you want now?

Gus   First it was blud, now, it's *you get me*?

Leslie   (*holds his crotch*)   See it deh? Jan's good for me that's all.

Gus   You know me, Les, as long as you are happy, I got your back.

Leslie   When Jonny Parsons chased me up Woolwich High Street with a Stanley, you and Trent standing there, pissing yourselves, that kind of having my back?

Gus   More like when I funded your rent for six months when you were on remand, that kind of having yer back.

Leslie   OK. Fair do's. (*Sips more champagne.*) This shit is proper nice.

Gus   Twelve motherfucking years, Les! Cha-rass!

Leslie   I predict a good night ahead.

Gus   As long as Selwyn reins it in.

Leslie   (*looks around the pub*)   Respect, Gus, you are doing well. Looks nice.

Gus   It will be if we ever get it finished. Toilets need looking at. A few more tiles to lay, English bwois too lazy, man. Eastern Europeans, however, know all about it. They know what a hard day work is. And Somalians. They don't know what a tea break is.

Leslie   Yeah, fuck minimum wage.

Gus   And I found another pub. Up in Blackheath. Right shit-hole from all accounts. Gonna do my magic there as well. From morning till night. Not one word of complaint from my workforce. Not one. Brexitards can kiss my arse.

Leslie   Yep, very well indeed.

Gus   She's good for you, this Mary.

Leslie   Jan!

Gus   It's what I said.

Leslie   You said Mary, yer cunt.

Gus   Well I meant Claire.

Leslie   Jan! Her name is Jan. *Dayz!*

Gus   'Dayz'? You saying *dayz* now?

Leslie   You want get merked?

Gus   That's it.

Leslie   Power down, big man.

Gus   *Blud! Dayz! Merked!* Why are you talking to me like a *younger*?

Leslie   I don't mean nothing by it, it ain't me.

Gus   Bloody sounds like you.

Leslie   It's this kid who I was sharing my room with at the hostel. He was coming out with all of it, *you get me, you low dat*, its infectious, what could I do?

Gus   You could have stopped.

Leslie   You know, I thought I had my feet well under the table there, my own room, telly, I felt like a lawd of my own creation. Well sweet. Then this cheeky little rass neck, straight out of some young offenders, shows up.

Gus   Oh yes, cheeky how?

Leslie   He kept moving my shoes around, you know what I am like with my shoes, Gus, with my things in fact, all of my things, I like them where I left them. I tell him to leave well enough alone, but all he does is grin, like it's meant to mean something.

He is about to turn on his e-cigarette.

Gus   By the door.

Leslie   It's a vape!

Gus   I don't business.

Leslie   Fuck's sake.

He stands by the door to have his smoke.

Gus   What was his play?

Leslie   Fucked if I know. I fronted him up a few times, respect your elders and that, but he denied all knowledge. He reckons it was the mice.

Gus   What a renk!

Leslie   Him and his grin. It was everything in me not to grab him by the throat and show him summin.

Gus   But you didn't though, Les?

Leslie   Do I look like I want to go back inside? Besides, he was big.

Gus   Big?

Leslie   Yeah, big. Not big as in fat, like Trent. I mean, he's stacked, can handle himself.

Gus   So what you are saying is, you were scared?

Leslie   I didn't say I was scared of the yout. I'm saying the yout was big.

Gus   So what if he was big?

Leslie   He could have a knife or summin.

Gus   I thought weapons weren't allowed in there?

Leslie   They're not allowed. But you could sneak one in, dead easy. The security in that place is a joke. The geezer at the front desk don't speak English, not a word of it.

Gus   So, you were scared of this yout?

Leslie   Not of him, but he might have had a knife.

Gus   Were you scared, Les, yes or no?

Leslie   I was scared of the knife, Gus, is that not allowed?

Gus   But he didn't have one.

Leslie   What are you now, Old Bill? He might have. But you know what the kids are like around here. They don't think they are summin, unless they are carrying summin.

Gus   'S right, just don't be telling me you were scared, Les. That you are getting soft in your old age.

Leslie   A minute ago, you said I shouldn't touch him. And less of the 'old', please?

Gus   You shouldn't touch him. But don't be scared to touch him, there's a difference.

Leslie   I was this much away from parking a chair into the side of his head. Good enough for yer? It took Claire two hours to calm me down one night.

Gus   You mean Jan!

Leslie   My bwoi.

Gus   Fuck off! If this kid's giving you bollocks, jog on out of there.

Leslie   No need, the kid's gone.

Gus   You can do better.

Leslie   I can't afford better. And go where exact? I can't move in with Jan, she'll lose her job.

Gus   You know where.

Leslie   I said no.

Gus   'Kin 'ell, Leslie. Not only do you choose to wine and dine yourself at the local food bank and not let me fund yer. You'd also rather sleep in some shite-hole hostel than one of my flats?

Leslie   Where our *wall* used to be?

Gus Here we go.

Leslie Remember the wall, Gus?

Gus You been thick?

Leslie We can't all be rich privileged wankers like you, can we? We're not allowed.

Gus Yes, thank you, *Jeremy Corbyn*.

Leslie Also, Jan's words were 'No associating with known criminals'.

Gus Is that what she sees me as? A 'known criminal'? Facety gal. Have I ever seen the inside of a courtroom? I don't think so! If thass she feel, what you doing here then?

Leslie A long overdue session with my bruvvers is one thing. Crashing at your poncy gaff where our beloved wall used to be –

Gus Shut up about the wall.

Leslie – is extracting the Michael a touch.

Gus Well, I am funding everything this evening, *everyting*! So just for tonight, for the love of Shaun, put yer pride away.

Leslie Yes, Dad!

Sound of knocking on the door.

Three knocks. We're on.

Gus Finally. Now, remember.

Leslie Yeah, yeah, no feely-feely, touchy-kissy, 'kin 'ell!

Gus Hold up a sec, I got it all set up to do this, watch me now, see it deh.

He turns on the jukebox. With merely the touch of a button, he presses it to play 'Glad All Over', sung by the Crystal Palace football team of 1990. He and **Leslie** *sing along.*

The door swings opens. It is **Trent***. They stop singing.*

Gus   Fuck's sake, Trent.

He turns off the jukebox.

Trent   Fuck's sake what?

Leslie   You lead him in first, we said.

Trent   I know what we said, but about that –

Leslie   Gwan then.

Gus   Where is he, parking?

Leslie   You got him parking your car, Trent?

Trent   Hold up.

Gus (*calls*)   Shaun? Shaun? Batty bwoi, ware yu deh?

Trent   Gus?

Gus   You had better not have been smoking skunk in your car again, what if you got pulled over, you woulda got him sent right back.

Trent   Gus?

Gus   Think it through, Trent.

Trent (*trying to get a word in*)   Gus, man –

Gus (*calls*)   Shaun? Where him deh?

Trent   I dunno.

Gus   Yer dunno.

Trent (*looks around*)   Nice yard, Jesusss!

Gus   Trent, where is Shaun?

Trent   Well, let me give it to you straight, Gus. *Mi. Nuh. Know!*

Gus   But you said you were bringing him.

Trent   I know what I said. I went to his muddda's yard as agreed, hardly my fault if he isn't there now.

Leslie   He had to be there.

Trent   Well, he ain't there.

Leslie   You call him?

Trent   Yeah, I *call* him. I had it all arranged and shit. He would head for his mum's after his release. I drive up there, bring his no-good, skinny white Irish arse back here.

Gus   So?

Trent   So, he wasn't there, Gus.

Gus   So where then?

Trent   I'm getting bored saying this, mi nuh rhatid know! Joke is, his mum ain't seen him neither.

Gus   What time did he go out?

Trent   You don't get what I am meaning, Gus.

Gus   Well, hurry up and mean then.

Trent   His mum ain't seen him at all, not since he got out.

Leslie   Bollocks.

Trent   Ask her. Go see her.

Gus   Well, that ain't right, that don't make any sense.

Trent   Believe it don't. His mum says the last time she see him was a week and a half ago, when she last visited him in the nick.

Leslie (*chuckles*)   You don't think they kept him in, do yer? That he done summin.

Gus   You mean hit a screw?

Leslie   It wouldn't be the first time, would it?

Gus   Only explanation.

Leslie   Stupid motha!

Gus   He can't hold it in.

Trent   Excuse?

Gus   I wonder what the screw say to get him all flared up?

Trent   Excuse?

Gus   Something about Palace, has to be.

Leslie   If that screw was Millwall.

Gus   No, don't. Cos that's just carnage, we are talking.

He and **Leslie** *chuckle at the thought.*

Trent   I said excuse?

Leslie   Giving it all that, like a lobster. Can you imagine?

Gus   Game over, cha rass.

Leslie   You know it.

Trent   Yo. Excuse me?

Gus   What, what you want?

Trent   A word if I may?

Gus   Gwan nuh!

Leslie   Keeping us hanging. Spit it out.

Gus   Rass!

Leslie   Innit!

Trent   Shaun was released. They bring his arse out yesterday, Just as they planned. No bother. No mention of Palace or Millwall. Happy? Two twos, the purest kind.

Leslie   You sure about this?

Trent   I checked with dem. He should have been there at his mum's, waiting for me, as per the plan.

Gus   This is a weird one. We had this planned, cha rass. You pick him up, soften him up with a couple of whiskeys. Plenty more here. A couple of sorts all paid for, ready and waiting to give him a proper PSE, right or wrong, Leslie?

Leslie   Pepsi and Shirlie! They've only got a website, can you believe?

Gus   Him gonna bruc some serious ass tonight. A few hours' sleep at a five-star if he is lucky, finally, the grand finale, a three p.m. kick-off at the Park. No way on planet Earth is Shaun missing any of that. He should be here, he wanted to be here, it mek no sense.

Leslie   You know him, he loves to piss about too much. He'll come charging through that door any moment, glad all over, asking, where Pepsi and Shirlie at?

Trent   Exactly. So, what you have for me, gents, cos I is gasping?

Gus (*points to the champagne*)   Gwan.

Trent *pours himself a glass.* **Leslie** *examines his waistline.*

Leslie   That's a fair bit of timber you got going on there, Trent. Diet not working for you again?

Trent (*holds his crotch*)   See it deh, suck it nuh. Lawd, mi need this. This is mate's rates, yeah?

Salut!

Gus/Leslie   Salut!

Trent *downs it in one.*

Trent   Ooh! This is the tits!

He has another.

Gus   Booze ain't going anywhere you know, Trent.

Trent   Blud, just let me drink yeah?

Gus   You as well?

Trent   Me as well, what?

Gus   Wid this *blud*?

Trent   Fuck is this?

Leslie   Leave it.

Trent   Trying to.

Gus   You alright there, Trent?

Trent   Yeah, man. I'm fine.

Gus   From the time you come in here, you look all out of breath.

Trent   It was nothing, I'm sweet.

Gus   What was nothing?

Trent   I said I was fine.

Gus   But you said it was nothing.

Trent   What was?

Gus   What de rass is wrong with everyone tonight? Straight answer to a straight question, two twos, Trent, what is up?

Trent   Nothing is up, nothing much.

Gus   Which is what? Tell me now before you get a slap so hard, your Zulu ancestors are going to feel it.

Trent   Just a little encounter I had on the way here.

Gus   An encounter?

Trent   Nothing for you to get the arsehole about. It was a couple of youngers.

Gus   Youngers?

Trent   Them ones from the estate, with their jeans down to their arses.

Leslie   Saggers.

Trent   Prancing around the manor like they own it.

Leslie   And they don't say manor, it's all postcodes now.

Trent   I know that, 'kin 'ell!

Gus   I don't give a rass what they call the manor.

Leslie   Endz. That's what they call it.

Gus   Did you not hear me say?

Leslie   Gus, it's all around man, it can't be helped. Like it or no, this is their turf.

Trent   Come on, you know this.

Leslie   Bit hard to Trent, him living in West Norwood and all.

Gus   West Dulwich, actually, if you must envy me all your life, get it right, Les.

Leslie   My bad.

Gus   Do they work? Do any of these jokers pay tax? A single penny of it? Talk to me, Trent, and don't say to me nuttin happened.

Trent   I was scoping the manor, looking for Shaun.

Gus   Yes?

Trent   I was stepping to my car, and these youngers were all hanging around the corner, like they were into summin. I almost walked into them, I caught eyes with one of dem, must be the big man, he gets in uptight saying he didn't like the way I was looking at him, that I was eyeballing him. I wasn't.

Gus   You weren't.

Trent   No.

Gus   But you said that, you said you weren't?

Trent   Yeah.

Gus   Why?

Trent   Why?

Gus   Why, Trent?

Trent   Gus, I don't know, I just did.

Leslie   Because he wasn't, Gus.

Gus   Weren't what?

Leslie   Eyeballing him for fuck!

Gus   Did you lay him out, Trent?

Trent   Gus, there was about eight of them.

Gus   So that would be a 'no' then?

Leslie   What did you expect him to do?

Gus   Go tell the yout summin about himself and his mum, at least.

Trent   I did do summin!

Gus   Yes, Trent, my boy, more like!

Trent   I asked him . . .

Gus   Say that again?

Trent   Told! I told him to step off.

Gus   You didn't ask?

Trent   What do you take?

Gus   What did you say?

Trent   You know.

Gus   No, I don't know.

Trent   'Mind yourself, young one. Grown-up walking, going about his business, so make a path for me, yeah?' Respect and that, the whole package, complete verbal.

Gus   And did they make a way for you?

Trent   Oh, why can't you just leave it, Gus?

Gus   Just look at me and answer the question. Did they make a way for you?

Trent   No, they didn't.

Gus   Fuck!

Trent   But I handled it, Gus. Hear me, fer trut.

Gus   Handle it how? How did you handle it?

Trent   Like I said, man!

Gus   They rough you up?

Trent   More of a jostle.

Gus   A jostle?

Trent   I didn't think it was worth the agg.

Leslie   You think right, Trent, you done good. It was not worth the agg. Hear him, Gus, now drink up. (*Toasts.*) To Shaun.

Trent   Gus?

Gus   That's my name.

Trent   We cool?

Gus   We cool. It's alright, Trent.

Leslie   Excellent, 'bout time. Now drink!

Gus   As long as you are sure, Trent.

Trent   You think I am lying to you now?

Leslie   Trent, he's fucking with yer.

Gus   You do not have a thing to worry about.

Sound of someone approaching the door.

Hear that?

Leslie   Told you, what did I say, he's fucking about.

Gus   Here we go.

He turns on the jukebox again to play 'Glad All Over'. They all sing along.

Doors open.

Leslie   Yes, Shaun!

Trent   You bastard, yu . . .

It is **Selwyn** *and* **Fraser**. **Selwyn** *hobbles in on one foot.*

Selwyn   I don't know how you arse bandits are mistaking me for Shaun.

Gus   Is this some fucking joke?

He turns off the jukebox.

Leslie   Where the rass is this guy?

Selwyn   Shaun ain't here?

Gus   Does it look? (*Recognises* **Fraser** *immediately.*) Well, ain't dis a bitch.

Wa gwan, Selwyn?

Selwyn   My nephew. He's alright. Innit, bwoi?

Fraser   Yeah, I am fine, thank you very much.

Gus   This is a big man party we have going here, Selwyn, tonight! I got my place all set up for everyone.

Selwyn   Real nice by the way.

Gus   But you bring some lickle yout to it?

Fraser   I'm twenty.

Selwyn   Whoa there, yungsta, cool yer jets. No mind him, Gus.

Fraser   I'm old enough to drink, I am a big boy, I can tek care of myself.

Gus   True say you can, cos I didn't hear anybody say you have permission to talk.

Selwyn   Mouth shut, younger. What did I tell you?

Gus   Is this you being fresh, young one?

Fraser   Nuh man.

Selwyn   Leave the yout, Gus. Please?

Fraser   I didn't mean no offence.

Selwyn   How about you just wait in the car for me, yeah?
Like I suggested to you in the first place?

Gus   You want him to stay in the car all night, Selwyn?

Selwyn   Well, it's kinda clear you do not want him here.

Gus   Did I say that? Trent, help me out here, did I say that?

Trent   Nuh man, you didn't.

Selwyn   Alright then.

Gus   You should really let the boy speak for himself yu nuh,
Selwyn.

Fraser   Look, I mean no disrespect. I would really like to
stay and hang with you guys, but I will go if you want me to.

Gus   What you tink, Les? Les? Earth calling Leslie?

Leslie   What, what you want?

Gus   Your attention on this if you don't mind.

Leslie   Fuck me, already.

Gus   What you have to say?

Leslie   I got nuttin to say.

Selwyn   His mind must be on the latest bit of ebony has
home waiting for him. That's what it is.

Gus   Ain't you heard, Sel? He is getting it on with his
probation officer.

Selwyn (*laughs out loud*)   Lawd Jesus!

Gus   He's a naughty boy, our Les.

Selwyn   A suit as well as an ebony. Gwan, Leslie!

Gus   She ain't no ebony.

Selwyn   Move yerself!

Leslie   You move!

Selwyn   No one love de black pum as well as you man, gw'y!

Leslie   I don't just like black, I don't know where the life of this is coming from, I really don't . . . Fucking hell and Jesus wept . . . she's a snowball.

Selwyn   White chick?

Leslie   Yes, Sel, white! So white, it mek you sick.

Selwyn   White don't mek me sick. Pum is pum mate, I ain't no racist.

Leslie   Well, I am happy to hear that, Sel, that makes me feel so much better about myself!

Selwyn   I don't know where you hear that from, that white makes me sick. No idea, at all.

Leslie   I happen to love her, alright?

Selwyn   Love?

Leslie   End of discussion, at least I hope it is. I really hope it is.

Gus   I know it's love, Les. Better believe it is love. You going off in a daydream like that. Gotta be love shit, the purest kind. Strongest kind, Celine Dion and all that.

Leslie   Oh, fuck off. See it deh.

Gus   (*to* **Fraser**) You want hang, hang, as long as you don't mind big man talk.

Fraser   The best kind.

Gus   So, which are you? Which one of Selwyn's sisters are you?

Selwyn   He don't come from that side, Gus. Two, twos, my dad's side he raise up in. That is where he come from. One of my dad's brother's kids or summin.

Gus   And does your dad brother's kid have a name?

Selwyn   Oh shame, only just realised. I didn't even say.

Gus   Well, you can say it now, can't you?

Fraser   Fraser.

Selwyn   Yes, yes, boys meet Fraser, Fraser, meet the boys.

Fraser   Pleased to meet, honoured to be here.

Gus   Honoured?

Fraser   Well, yeah. It's ca it is you, I mean it is you, all of you in fact. It is, innit?

Gus   Innit what, what is?

Fraser   You're the firm right?

Gus   And what you think you know about our firm?

Fraser   Legends! Each and every one a' you.

Gus   So what bring you here?

Fraser   Just helping Selwyn here out, my uncle.

Gus   Out?

Selwyn (*holding up cans of beer*)   Wid these for one. This is a party, yes?

Gus   This is also a pub, as you can see.

Fraser   Yeah. I can see, nice.

Gus   Why you bringing a crate of beer to my yard, Sel?

Selwyn   I dunno, I just thought.

Gus   You didn't think.

Selwyn   We're having a session; we always have beer for a session.

Gus   Look at my bar, look around. I got the grand opening tomorrow night. But I wanted you here, I wanted my boys to be here. We had it all planned. Why don't you listen to me, why don't you ever listen to me?

Selwyn   Alright, man, sorry. Calm it down.

Fraser   Still a party though, yeah?

Leslie   With no guest of honour.

Fraser   Unlucky.

Selwyn   Come, Fraser. Back in a sec. We got more beers in the car. Well, we might as well bring them in. Dat alright, Gus?

Gus   Gwan den.

Selwyn   Come, Fraser.

Fraser *follows* **Selwyn** *out.*

Gus   I got enough drink flowing, and he brings beer!

Leslie   Take your tampon out, Gus, listen.

Gus   What?

Leslie   That's him.

Gus   Who, what, when, who?

Leslie   This kid Selwyn just bring in. Large as life. It's him.

Gus   Gonna need more than that, bruv.

Leslie   The kid I shared the room with. At the hostel! The yout!

Gus   Who him?

Leslie   I couldn't believe it at first.

Gus   For real?

Leslie   Breezing himself right in here, like he doesn't know me.

Gus   The same little fucker that was taking your shoes?

Leslie Hiding my shoes.

Gus But him that?

Leslie Yes.

Gus Him?

Leslie Him, Gus, him!

Gus Well, this is interesting.

Leslie He must have a game going on.

Gus Well, obviously. Breezing himself in here like he's summin. And him see you too. And he must know that. What kind of nonsense is this? We go find out what it is. His game.

Leslie Well, whatever it is, just leave me out of it.

Gus Leave you out of it?

Leslie Whatever it is.

Gus What the fuck are you going on about, whatever it is, Leslie? I haven't even done nothing yet, I ain't made a move or nuttin, am just merely speaking out loud and shit.

Leslie Come on, Gus, we know how it go.

Gus Oh really, Leslie, and what might that be? You tell me how it go?

Leslie I don't want no trouble.

Gus What trouble? Why do you think I want to do summin? I tell you, Leslie, you really are on a one-way ticket train ride to being a fully paid-up prime-time pussy, innit? This Claire . . .

Leslie Jan!

Gus It's what I said.

Leslie You said Claire.

Gus Oh fuck what her name is. Point is, you are well under manners!

Leslie   Yes, Gus, and I am loving it.

Gus   A shit yu a talk!

Leslie   Mind yer own.

Gus   You want focus here? Yes, or no? This kid has me curious. Him show up here. You know him. With all that, you are not in the slightest?

Leslie   Nope.

Gus   Pussy den.

Leslie   I'm sorry I opened my mouth.

Gus   Just answer me these two things, Les. Just two things. Why don't you wanna know what this little boy's game is?

Leslie   I don't want trouble. I'm done with that life. I promised Jan.

Gus   I don't see her here.

Leslie   A promise is a promise. You taught me that.

Gus *sucks his teeth.*

Leslie   Right. Second question?

Gus   For as long as we have both known Trent, coming on forty years if you can believe that, for as long as we can remember, I never known him to keep his mouth shut about anything. This is one brer who has made a religion of putting his nose in other people's business.

Leslie   What's the question, Gus?

Gus   Here's the question. Don't you think it's a little peculiar he has kept his mouth shut for so long, he ain't stepped in or anything like that, even now, when we are chatting his name?

Leslie   Alright, I give you that, that is strange.

They both look towards **Trent***.*

Gus   Trent?

Trent   Lawd, Jesus.

Gus   He speaks! You have something to say to me, Trent? Do I want to hear it?

Trent   Yes, and no. But mostly, no.

Gus   I'm intrigued already. Come then.

Trent   The youngers I was having trouble with, earlier today, he was one of them.

Gus   Come again?

Trent   He was one of them boys, he had the biggest mouth as well.

Gus   How can you be so sure?

Trent   He got into my face, Gus.

Gus   The one who accuse you of eyeballing him? Him dat?

Trent   The very same, Gus, the one and only, without a doubt. The slightest!

Gus   Yes, alright, Trent.

Trent   You asked, you wanted to know, why I was all quiet.

Gus   Yes, now I can't get you to shut up. Let me think, nuh? Les?

Leslie   What now?

Gus   Are you just going to stand there, and go all silent again?

Leslie   Alright, then, it's ripe. What else you want me to say?

Gus   Some lickle yout is having his way with two of my boys? He has some jokes!

Selwyn *comes back in, carrying more beers.*

Selwyn   No, you are alright, boys. Don't even worry about giving the cripple a hand, you all just stand there like you case is about to come up. Trent, you've been putting on a bit of timber there, bro.

Trent (*sighs*)   And here it come.

Selwyn   Is it that hard to take the skin off the chicken? Hungry fer trut.

Trent   Why don't you go away and grow yourself a foot?

Selwyn (*grabs his own crotch*)   See mi foot deh?

Gus   Tell me about this kid of yours.

Selwyn   Not my kid, I know we all look alike.

Leslie (*chants*)   Oh, racist!

Gus   Alright then, this younger. Tell me about him.

Selwyn   I have told you.

Gus   I don't think you have, man.

Selwyn   Yes, I did. He's from my dad's side.

Gus   That's my point, Sel. I don't think he is a relation of yours.

Selwyn   Of course he is.

Gus   You sure about, no offence?

Selwyn   None taken, he's my blood, Gus, why would he lie about that?

Leslie   Yes, Sel, why would he lie?

Gus   You have officially got me and my head going, Selwyn.

Selwyn   Look, our paths crossed a few weeks back, at work of all places!

Trent   He work with you at the supermarket, Selwyn?

Selwyn   You don't have to say like that you know, Trent.

Trent   Like what, you fool?

Selwyn 'The supermarket'!

Trent Oh cha!

Selwyn Like I should be ashamed.

Trent Well, are you?

Selwyn It's a motherfucking job, so step.

Gus Hey!

Trent One question is all I ask.

Gus Trent!

Trent And he gets the arsehole like always.

Selwyn Yer fat fucker, yu.

Trent (*holds his crotch*) See it deh?

Gus Are the two of you done? Selwyn, tell me about this yout?

Leslie Two twos, Sel.

Selwyn Alright. Like I was saying, we met at work. He was shopping and shit, saw me, then stepped towards. Telling me he thinks we are related and shit I ask how, he explains he is my Uncle Carl's middle son, from his first marriage. He gimme dates and stats, all seem pucker, above board and that.

Leslie You never gave a fart about your dad's lot.

Selwyn I still don't.

Gus So, why you reach for him?

Selwyn Business of course, what else?

Leslie Business?

Selwyn The best kind, the kind of business we do, or at least we used to.

Leslie Did it ever occur to you, Selwyn, he may have found out all that shit about yer family?

Selwyn   Yes, thank you, Leslie, it did.

Leslie   A lie you a' tell, man.

Selwyn (*holds his crotch*)   See it deh, suck it nuh!

Gus   What is this, are we fucking infants now?

Selwyn   It did occur, but why lie? What is there to be gained from that, someone, tell me?

Gus   You said business?

Selwyn   Yeah, man, big business.

Gus   Not the same business that you have been going on and on about, Selwyn?

Selwyn   I brought him here because I thought you need persuading.

Gus   Are you telling me this is the boys' ting?

Leslie   He don't look a day over eighteen, Sel. And him tink he bright already?

Selwyn   I know; I couldn't believe it first when I hear him chat. We are talking some serious wedge here, Gus.

Trent   How much?

Gus   Oh, he speaks again! You want in now, Trent?

Trent   I want to hear first, is that not allowed?

Gus   You should want in to buss this kid's head in.

Selwyn   For what?

Gus   Tell him.

Trent   Me and this kid of yours we had a run-in, earlier today.

Leslie   Him and some youngers were troubling him.

Trent   They weren't troubling me!

Leslie   It's what you said.

Trent   He didn't like the way I eyeballed him. That's it. End of.

Selwyn   Why are you surprised?

Gus   Surprised?

Selwyn   Well, they are all like that these days

Gus   Is this you defending them, Selwyn?

Selwyn   I am only stating a fact, Gus.

Gus   A fact, is it now?

Selwyn   Alright then not a fact merely an observation. An observation about what these youts like to go on wid.

Gus   The kind of youths who do supermarkets, Selwyn?

Selwyn   Yes.

Gus   The kind of youts round that know nothing apart burn up shop in Charlton and teif shoe, cha rass!

Selwyn   That nonsense was six years ago, Gus, it was nothing worse than what we done. Brixton '85, anyone?

Trent   Now, that was a session.

Leslie   Yeah, an entire fleet of Maggie's boys chasing us up Brixton Hill.

Trent   We gave them a spanking.

Leslie   They gave us a spanking.

Selwyn   About the boy, I say he is alright. He rolls with the BMC.

Gus   The what? Who?

Selwyn   Bare Money Crew. They're the top firm around here.

Gus   Oh, are they now?

Selwyn   He's their top boy.

Gus   What, him? Oh, do me one, will yer?

Selwyn   I asked around, he checks out.

Gus   Stop before you cream yourself. (*To* **Leslie** *and* **Trent**.) Any of this mek sense to you?

Trent   BMC are hardcore, Gus.

Gus   So, what do the BMC want wid us, ca' they deh fucking up my night here.

Trent (*calls*)   Come on, Shaun, anytime now, mate!

Leslie   You sure he's on the level, Sel?

Selwyn   Word is, yeah.

Leslie   Word is? Don't you know for sure?

Selwyn   How am I supposed to know for sure?

Leslie   Ask around nuh?

Selwyn   What do you think I did?

Leslie   You said 'word is'. Sounds like you were playing Chinese whispers or summin.

Selwyn   I was told, by those on the in, he's a top boy. What more you want? Gus, all I am saying to you is hear him out?

Gus   Saying? Sounds like you begging to me, Selwyn.

Trent   True dat.

Selwyn   Trent, could you spend one day without kissing Gus's arse? Do you think that it's possible? Just one?

Trent   Tek yer pills, yu nuthead.

Selwyn   Gus? You go hear him out, man?

Gus   Oh, I will, backwards and forwards, cover to cover, will I hear him out. I'm gonna weigh him in. Ware him deh?

Selwyn   He's still outside. He had to take a call.

Gus   Well, unless it's Rihanna him chat to, it's time he wrapped it up, bring his arse in for me. Like right now, Sel.

Selwyn   Yeah, on it, man.

He goes.

Gus   Gonna get to the bottom of this fun and games, that's for sure.

Leslie   Careful now, Gus, you might start enjoying this shit again.

Gus   Livvy got ghosted out from the Scrubs, right?

Leslie   Six months ago.

Gus   You think he might know where Shaun is at?

Leslie   Shaun weren't in Scrubs wid him that long.

Gus   Call him anyway. See if he knows anything.

Fraser *follows* **Selwyn** *in carrying more beer.*

Fraser   Dayz, bruv, you have enough here for a week, let alone a night.

He can feel all eyes on him.

Summin I can help you wid?

Gus   Is there a problem you have, Fraser?

Fraser   A problem?

Gus   Yes, you yungsta, do you have a problem here?

Fraser   Do you think I have a problem, Gus?

Gus   Sorry, I forget. You don't like being eyeballed, do you, Fraser?

Fraser   Say? Sorry?

Gus   Nuh, man, it is I who should be sorry. Seeing as you are Selwyn's family and that. We ain't had a proper intro and shit.

I'm Gus. This is Trent, who you met earlier today, and of
course you know Leslie, seeing as the two were room buddies.

Selwyn   Say what?

Fraser   Oh, didn't I say?

Selwyn   No you rhatid well didn't.

Fraser   Did you ever find your shoe yet, Leslie?

Selwyn   Alright, what is this, wa gwan, younger?

Fraser   Nothing much.

Gus   Nothing much, he says.

Leslie   I don't like people touching my shoes.

Gus   And Trent. Tell him about Trent.

Selwyn   Yes, tell me about Trent.

Fraser   Just a couple of my brers trying it on.

Trent   You all bloody were.

Fraser   Just messing bredren, nothing personal, I swear.
I could see how upset you were.

Trent   Now hold up.

Fraser   I told them all to dial it down, didn't you hear?

Gus   You never said that, Trent.

Trent (*panicking*)   I know!

Fraser   None of them meant to make you feel afraid, Trent.

Trent   Afraid?

Gus   You said.

Trent   Yes, Gus, I know.

Gus   So yes or fucking no then, Trent? Were you scared?

Trent   No.

Gus   So, how come he?

Trent   I can't help what this younger is going wid.

Fraser   Maybe I should go?

Gus   Maybe you should stay right where you are, younger. And I mean, right there.

Fraser   If you insist.

Leslie   Oh he does. Best not forget.

Fraser   I didn't, I wasn't, I mean look at you, Durnfield boys, every one of you. Top-notch firm in all of South.

Gus   I know it can't be just me, but I can't help but feel you are tekin the piss a little.

Fraser   What do you think?

Gus   I am thinking that you have a game here.

Fraser   Good one, is there more?

Gus   You make a move on Leslie, then you start on Trent, now Selwyn. What is it about us you find so fascinating? What up wid that?

Fraser   I don't mean no disrespect. I just wanted to know what you lot were all about, that's all.

Selwyn   Tell me summin, are we fam or not?

Fraser   Do we even look like fam?

Selwyn   I thought so, especially around the eyes.

Fraser   Give it up, Selwyn, I played you.

Gus   So, why?

Fraser   Why do you think, Gus?

Selwyn   Yer lucky I don't hand you yer own arse.

Fraser *laughs.*

Gus   Boy thinks it joke!

Fraser   Well, it was, wasn't it? I mean no offence, Selwyn, but I don't fight cripples.

Trent   True say you don't know Selwyn, innit Gus? They don't call Sel crunch fer nuttin.

Gus   You know why they call him Sel crunch, boy?

Fraser   I think I am about to.

Gus   Whenever we tooled up for an encounter, a session –

Leslie   And there was many.

Gus   Selwyn here would have the guy down, and he would crunch, not bite, but crunch the brer's ear. Do you know what an ear looks like when it gets crunched by Selwyn? Like a cornflake.

Fraser   That's some nastiness, right there.

Gus   Is that all you can say?

Fraser   I needed to get close, meeting Leslie was coincidental. I couldn't believe it at first. It was like God's way of saying, I should do this ting.

Gus   What *ting*?

Fraser   I chose to make it personal with you, Selwyn, sorry. Look, I know we can do some business together.

Gus   The job?

Leslie   The same job you have been talking Gus's ear off about, Sel? No one does supermarkets any more. If you knew us all as well as you claim, you would know we never did. That shit wasn't for us.

Fraser   You never took things that didn't belong to yer? You were a bunch of fucking teifs.

Gus   You wanna watch yer mout for me?

Fraser   Are you telling or asking?

Gus   True talk now, supermarket is a joke, yes? It has to be.

Fraser   I never said supermarket. Selwyn, what you bin saying, man?

Selwyn   Move yourself from me now.

Fraser   Not a problem.

Selwyn (*warns*)   Hear me.

Trent   I beg you. younger, hear him.

Fraser   Hard not to.

Gus   If it's not a supermarket, then what? What is it?

Fraser   It's a woman.

Gus   A woman?

Fraser   Let me explain.

Gus   I think you had better.

Fraser   She works in the supermarket, same one as Sel.

Selwyn   Selwyn to you.

Fraser   Every Friday, Selwyn says he sees her, putting all the takings together. It should be two of them working in the office, but it's run by a couple of Sikhs, too tight-fisted to have someone working with her, leaving her on her own, a woman. By the time she gets around to it, there must be about ten grand in there at least. Woman is one dem you know . . .

Gus   No, I don't know.

Fraser   Scared ones, innit, Sel? Selwyn. You said.

Gus   Never mind Sel, carry on.

Fraser   One a' dem, who clutch their handbags like their life depended on it whenever they see us. So you know?

Gus   Know what?

Fraser   We go in and we reach her. One look from us and she will give it up, quick smart.

Gus   And what if she doesn't?

Fraser   She will.

Gus   But what if she doesn't, Fraser?

Fraser   She will.

Gus   I am getting so arse-bored with people not answering my questions tonight, what if she doesn't? What would you expect us to do then?

Fraser   What do you think?

Gus   Tell me.

Fraser   Come on, you know.

Gus   No, I don't know.

Fraser   Well, you shut her up, innit?

Leslie   Shut her up?

Fraser   Yes.

Gus   You mean hurt her? You want us to hurt this woman, is that right, Fraser?

Fraser   It won't come to that.

Gus   Yes or no, my young friend, if she, this woman, can't keep her tail quiet, do you expect us to hurt her?

Fraser   Well yeah. Alright then, yeah. I expect you to handle the bitch.

Gus   Mind yerself.

Fraser   I expect you to hurt her. I expect you to shut her mouth and keep it shut for her. Is that clear enough for you?

Gus   Tell me summin. What exactly do you think should be happening to you, right now?

Fraser   I am not here to make a fool of you. We all know how much of a legend you are in these parts. Before you went legit. How many businesses you own now?

Leslie Six, that we know of.

Gus Never mind me, young one. It's the brers behind me.

Fraser OK then, you all have reps this big.

Trent Believe that.

Fraser I have to say though, I ain't impressed.

Gus *delivers a hard blow in* **Fraser***'s stomach.* **Fraser** *drops like a heap.*

Leslie Jesus, Gus!

Gus You impressed yet? You didn't see that coming right, not a whiff.

Trent Yes! How you feel now, bitch?

Fraser*, completely winded by that punch, struggles to breathe.*

Gus Get up, bwoi, carrying on like it hurt. Don't make a big ting about this yeah?

Leslie You'll be alright, yungsta, just tek a breather, yeah?

Fraser Fuck off, man.

Leslie Hey mind yerself.

Fraser You mind yerself! We brers or summin?

Trent Listen, like he's the dogs.

Gus Coming in here, of all nights, to my place, a special night for us, insulting our ears with some dumb-arse plan! You ain't no top boy! BMC, don't mek me laugh. If yer so hard core, how come you ain't reached for me yet? I just put you down, bwoi, but instead of flinging yerself at me, yu stand there like yer about to cry or something, gw'y!

Fraser That's gonna cost you, nigga.

The air in the room freezes

Gus Bwoi, you have any idea how many tear-ups we've had over the years, with mouthy skinheads with gobs this big, that we introduced to the business end of a piece of two-by-four timber, who couldn't shut up from calling us that? And don't even get me started on Maggie's boys.

Selwyn   So who are you then? (*Rages.*) From which blood claart you creep down from?

Trent   Sel?

Gus   On yer way bwoi, now.

Fraser   That's not very nice, Gus.

Gus   Move.

Selwyn   I wanna know first.

Gus   No, you don't.

Leslie   I thought you wanted to know what his play is.

Gus   Bwoi nuttin but a joke, man.

Fraser   Is that why, Gus? Is that why, ca I was a joke. Or was it cos I was a mistake? That's what yu said to her, innit?

Leslie   Her?

Gus   Bwoi, don't mek me tell yu again.

Selwyn   Who's yer mudda?

Fraser   Tell him, Gus.

Gus   Will you just forget dis fool.

Selwyn   Who, fer fuck . . . ?

Leslie   Come, bwoi, show us some brief.

Fraser   Tina Hardy. Ring a bell to any of you?

Trent   Tina Hardy?

Leslie   Sam's sister? You were on it wid her, Gus?

Gus   I was on it wid a whole heap, how am I supposed to remember?

Leslie   Are you winding me up? Sam Hardy's lickle sister, Gus?

Gus   What about her?

Leslie   The one who got herself up the spout when she was still at school, that was you? Gus, answer me nuh, was that you?

Trent   Dis yer yout, Gus? Him yer bwoi?

Gus   He ain't nuttin to me.

Fraser   That I do know.

Leslie   Why didn't you tell us straight up?

Selwyn (*to* **Fraser**)   Why didn't you tell me?

Gus   More to the point, Selwyn, you didn't tek one look at this bwoi and realise this was jokes? Did they amputate your brain as well as your foot?

Trent   Soff!

Gus   Soff? I don't know what the H you are coming out wid big man?

Trent   Gus, what?

Gus (*mocks*)   Gus, what? Getting all scared and shit ca some lickle yout's face you off!

Trent   I wasn't afraid.

Gus   So you say, so you lie. And Leslie?

Leslie   Yes, my turn.

Gus   Like you know it all.

Leslie   What's your question now, Gus?

Gus   You don't have summin to say, come on, white boy, speak to me.

Leslie   Leave me the fuck alone.

Gus   You is soff!

Leslie   She was fifteen.

Gus   She was sixteen, nearly.

Leslie   You were twenty-eight.

Gus   We did nothing wrong.

Leslie   You sure?

Gus   What's yer beef, man? I had time for Tina.

Trent   True say you did.

Gus   She was bright.

Leslie   You mean she was fit.

Gus   We're done talking about her, understood?

Fraser (*mocks*)   The Durnfield boys!

Gus   You feel like getting hurt again?

Trent   Must be.

Fraser   You are such a tough man, Trent, especially when you are standing near Gus, you fat bastard. Is that why you let yourself go, cos you couldn't compete?

Trent (*snaps*)   One more jibe about my weight, yeah?

Gus   Trent?

Trent   From anybody! One more!

Gus   Selwyn, while this lickle fassyhole is still breathing and able to walk, take his rass neck back to wherever you find him and keep him deh. Leslie, hello, you call Livvy yet?

Leslie   I got a text, he ain't seen him.

Gus   Find Gerry then. Call Gerry. Gerry Cleary, Les.

Leslie   Yeah, I know who Gerry is, Gus, thank you. (*Points to* **Fraser**.) But aren't you forgetting summin?

Gus   Sel, did I not say throw this boy's arse out?

Leslie   Is he yours or not?

Gus   I don't blasted know. Maybe.

Leslie   I don't see what the problem is.

Gus   You never do, mate.

Leslie   If he's yer bwoi, claim him for fuck

Fraser   Yeah, come on, Gus, claim me.

Gus   This bwoi!

Selwyn   Him an eeeedyat!

Fraser   Yes, well this eeeedyat have your attention now, innit?

Gus *goes for* **Fraser** *again.*

Fraser   Come then, finish me off, I promise you, the biggest mistake you will make, nigga!

Selwyn   Enough wid that word.

Fraser   What, 'nigga'?

Gus   Bitch mout like yer mudda.

Leslie   Him yer bwoi? Yes or no? Just say it, Gus.

Gus   Alright, him mine, so what?

Trent   You is Sam Hardy's nephew? Lawd Jesus!

Gus   I thought you went over the river, live by Chiswick way?

Fraser   Mum move back six months ago to care for Sam. I grew up hearing stories about you, how he rolled with you lot, the firm! Long before he had Aunty Sharon and Mum wiping his arse for him, that is.

Leslie   So, why didn't you tell us straight up who you were?

Fraser   Well, seeing the way you all left things with Sam when you last see him, I thought that was obvious. One minute the lot of you are tight as a drum, the next he gets mashed up in the head, and none of you go visit him in hospital, or at home. I mean, what is that?

Gus   Grown-up tings.

Selwyn   So about this supermarket?

Gus   Lawd Jesus, Sel, there is no supermarket.

Selwyn   I work there.

Gus   We ain't no harming no woman.

Selwyn   Who said anything about harming her, you heard what the boy said.

Gus   Are you sure? You want to up your dosage, Sel.

Fraser   I say it can work.

Gus   Who tell you to speak, you have a say?

Fraser   Sel is in, who else? Les?

Leslie   I am more curious that you did not tell us about Tina. Not a whiff, Gus.

Gus   Him my bwoi, we have the same blood, what more you want?

Fraser   Thanks for that.

Leslie   Schoolgirl or no, when she started to grow a pair, nearly every bro in the manner had half a mind to get it on wid that.

Fraser   You know I am standing right here.

Gus   She was a kid, Les.

Leslie   That didn't seem to stop you. In fact, I seem to recall you warning the entire firm that no one goes near, no one even thinks. Yet you slide on in without saying a word?

Gus   Yes, Les, summin like that.

Fraser   So, we go do dis ting?

Gus   Some one tek this bwoi out before I do summin.

Leslie   We don't hurt civilians, Fraser, we never did.

Selwyn   Not exactly true is it, though, Les?

Gus   Selwyn, shut up, man.

Fraser   Say?

Selwyn   It's ca' of what happened, innit?

Leslie   Sel!

Selwyn   It's why you want me to shut up?

Fraser   What happened?

Gus   Nuttin.

Trent   Leave it, boy.

Fraser   I want know.

Selwyn   I don't see a boy here, I see man, and he want know.

Gus   Sel, tek yer arse and sit down. (*To* **Fraser**.) And you, I'm gonna give you ten seconds to jog on.

Fraser   Bit late in the day for you to be barking orders.

Gus   Five seconds.

Selwyn   This is about the betting shop.

Leslie   Shut yer mout, Sel!

Selwyn   I thought we were done with that shit. I thought we were past that.

Fraser   You chatting about Sam's betting shop? The time he got robbed? Oh my . . . Was that you lot?

Gus   No, it wasn't us lot, it was this lot.

Leslie   Here it comes. Again!

Gus   Nuttin but a bunch of damn stupid eddyatts.

Leslie   Sam wasn't supposed to be there, what do you want? (*To* **Fraser**.) He wasn't supposed to be there, yungsta.

Trent   It was proper madness; we were going on wid back then.

Fraser   You know, Aunty Sharon always had a feeling you lot had summin to do with that.

Gus   So, what you want, we say sorry, summin like that?

Fraser   I couldn't give two licks about that place, or Sam for that matter. I barely know him. He'd come in and out of my life like a cold. I only had time for him was when he would tell me about rolling with you lot. Happiest days of his life, so I could never understand, for the life, how he gave up everything wid you, to open blasted bookies! You shoulda slapped him hard when he was coming out with that noise. How could he give you up? Shoulda slapped him. Hard!

Leslie   He's paying for it now, don't you think?

Fraser   I don't give a fuck.

Leslie   You didn't rate him?

Fraser   How could I rate a man like that?

Gus   But you rate us?

Fraser   Remains to be seen.

Gus   Do the job yerself if yu tink yer so bright.

Fraser   I need summin.

Gus   What that, a hug?

Fraser   A rep.

Gus   You want a rep?

Fraser   Wid the BMC fer fuck.

Leslie   We thought you rolled with them?

Gus   That you lead dem?

Fraser   Can be and will be. If we do dis ting, they are bound to recruit me, they will have to.

Gus   Well. I have heard all shit now.

Fraser   You owe me, bredren.

Gus   Don't call me bredren. I don't owe you jack.

Fraser   Come on, Sel, I know yer game.

Gus   You don't speak to him.

Selwyn   You don't speak for me, Gus.

Gus   You want do this shit? For real?

Selwyn   Maybe I need to

Gus   You don't need to, no one needs to, not that bad.

Selwyn   I do, Gus.

Gus   When have I ever not funded you, Sel. When have I ever not sorted you out large, for anyting?

Selwyn   Fuck yer funds, Gus.

Leslie   Power down, nuh.

Selwyn   Leave me alone, Les. This ain't about you, Gus.

Gus   So what then? Wa' gwan.

Selwyn   That blood-claart supermarket, and everyone in it. It's graft man, fer trut. 'Excuse me, I said excuse? Tell me which way it is to the deli counter.' They don't even bother asking, they don't even say please? 'Do you have fromage frais, light fromage frais I should say?' 'Would you mind going into your store room to see if you have any fennel left.' 'I went to the aisle as you said, but I still cannot find a can of pulses, only butter beans and chickpeas. I asked for pulses, do you even know what they are?' Listen yeah, I don't give a fucking blue-arsed rass about yer can of pulses, fuck yer can of pulses! Fuck it! Fuck off out of my face wid yer pulses. Tek yer pulses and ram dem up yer hole, bitch! You know how much dough me and my firm earned on a good day, bitch, enough to buy us a shop full of pulses, each! So step now before you know what is fucking good. Gus, it is everything in me not to tell them about themselves, every rhatid day! Tha, my friend, is *what gwan*.

Trent   Sel, come on, think this shit through.

Selwyn   You know, you ain't so bright these days yu nuh, Trent?

Trent   What?

Selwyn   When was the last time you grafted, and I mean serious grafting?

Trent   I'm doing alright.

Selwyn (*mocks*)   Doing alright! When was the last time you had some proper corn in the palm of your hand, Trent?

Fraser   We're talking ten large here, Trent.

Trent   We don't hurt people, Sel.

Fraser   You hurt Sam. Corn is corn, right? That's all there is, that what it's all about. You want it, you know you want it, you are sweating all over for it.

Leslie   Listen to him chat so, Gus's bwoi.

Gus   He ain't my bwoi.

Fraser   Gotta be worth a try, Leslie?

Leslie   My turn now?

Fraser   What do you have so bright, that you pass up this?

Gus   A woman.

Fraser   She must be some woman for you to look yer nose down on ten large.

Leslie   There are a hundred other ways to earn yourself a rep, Fraser.

Fraser (*defensive*)   Yeah, I know.

Leslie   Yet you choose this one.

Fraser   One wid less risks, no one gets hurt.

Gus   Where have I heard that before?

Leslie *goes behind the bar, pours out a couple of whiskey shots.*

Gus   Pardon fucking me, Les, but Les, what you doing?

Leslie   Pouring your boy a drink, man. And don't tell me
you don't drink, you want play wid man, right here so. Step
up. Show me summin.

Fraser *downs his shot in one. Then another.*

Fraser   Bring it.

Leslie *pours another.* **Fraser** *downs it again.* **Fraser** *wants another.*

Leslie   You sure?

Fraser   Are you lame or summin?

Leslie *pours one more.* **Fraser** *downs it again.*

Gus   Well that's OK then. Boy turn man now. He get a bit
of hair on his chest. So, let's all go out and do this ting. Yeah!
Never mind the fact it's a dumb-arse plan, and we find
ourselves back inside again.

Leslie   Again?

Gus   Doing at least ten years' bird.

Leslie   You've never done time, Gus.

Gus   So, what you telling me, Les, you want this to go tits up,
so it will be a first for me?

Leslie   Who said I was going along? I'm with you, bruv, it's
a shirt-arse plan. Two grand a man? That won't even keep you
in cufflinks. I'm just getting to know yer boy here. I just want
to know, why you never told us about you and Tina?

Gus   I don't know why.

Leslie   A lie yu a' tell.

Trent   The only time you keep shit to yourself is when it's too important to you.

Gus   Oh, is that right, Trent, thank you for making that so clear to me.

Leslie   Is that what it was, Gus, Tina was important to you?

Fraser   So important, I ain't seen his arse for fifteen years.

Leslie   'Seen'?

Gus   The fun's over, boy.

Leslie   Hold up. (*To* **Fraser**.) How old are you?

Fraser   I'm old enough, yeah,

Leslie   How old?

Fraser   Twenty.

Leslie   So, the last time you see him, you were five?

Gus   Is there a point coming this year, Les?

Leslie   You didn't tell us.

Gus   I think we have established that.

Leslie   Not only did you fool around wid Tina –

Gus   It wasn't like that.

Leslie   – but you had a yout wid her, a yout you knew about.

Fraser   He took me out sometimes.

Gus   Who tell you to speak?

Fraser   The park, I remember the park.

Trent   Durnfield Park?

Leslie   You never told us.

Gus   Get off it, Les.

Fraser   We would play football, one on one. I remember, he got me a football top. It must have been my birthday or summin.

Leslie   Your birthday?

Gus (*warns*)   Les?

Trent   What football top was it?

Selwyn   The next two words that leave your lips had better be Crystal Palace.

Fraser   What you take me for, Sel?

Selwyn   Hear him call me Sel now!

Fraser   I'm an Eagle through and through.

Selwyn   'S right then, as long as we are clear. On the same page.

Gus   We are nowhere near on the same page here.

Leslie   That is no way to talk your yout, Gus, now is it?

Fraser   Am used to it.

Gus   What him say? Used to it?

Fraser   Used to you not being around.

Gus   Oh man, fuck off with that please?

Fraser   You told her you were bored, you had yer fun, didn't want to know, yes or no?

Gus   Oh well, then it must be true then.

Leslie   You said it weren't like that.

Gus   Why don't you find out where Shaun is instead of digging your nose in my business?

Trent   At least you made him a Palace boy. You got that right.

Gus   As opposed to what, Trent?

Trent   I dunno, Gus, sometimes I feel –

Gus   Feel what?

Trent   That you're Millwall in disguise.

Gus (*holds his crotch*)   See it deh, suck it nuh.

Fraser   Oh man, this is it, innit?

Trent   This is what?

Gus   What you want now?

Fraser   The banter. Sam said you were all full of it, you could go at it all night long. On the *wall*.

Selwyn   The *wall*!

Trent (*reminisces*)   Our fucking *wall*, man.

Leslie   They knocked it down

Trent   I know they knock it down, I got eyes, Les.

Leslie (*grabs his crotch*)   See it deh!

Fraser   Tell me about it, tell me about the *wall*? While we are waiting for Shaun.

Gus   We? Four shots of Rémy, don't mek yu a man yu nuh, it doesn't mek you one of us.

Fraser   Aright, whilst *yer* waiting for Shaun, better fer you?

Gus   Don't let me tump yu again, yungsta.

Fraser   No way will I let you.

Gus   Leave now, whilst you can.

Leslie   He ain't going anywhere.

Gus   I don't want to hear one more sound of pussy talk coming from you, Leslie, you hear me?

Leslie   He's yer bwoi, I want to know him, even if you don't. How's that for pussy talk?

Gus   Well, Leslie has some jokes tonight.

Leslie   Tell Fraser about the *wall*, Trent.

Trent   Why me?

Leslie   Ca' you were there first, tell him.

Fraser   Oh yes, come on, gimme a tale.

Trent   The *wall* was our life; you understand? From the top of Albert Street Park till where the old church is. That four-foot high, forty-feet long, beautiful fucking *wall*, man. I'm eleven years old, first day of my new school, as I stepped in, I see Shaun. And he wants to fight me. I don't know why, I never clapped eyes on him before but he wants to fight me.

Selwyn   He just didn't like the look of yer.

Trent   He was the school crazy. Every school had one, and he was ours. It was my first day, I didn't want to fight, get my uniform all torn up, fucking hell. But I'm on his radar, he's got me in his sights, how do I get out of this, I thought, then my big sister steps in.

The guys laugh as they remember this.

Donna, God rest her soul. As big as me, my family, we are all built. We're stacked. She gives him one tump and he goes flying. Now, it was the first day at school, like I said.

Gus   Two twos, Trent.

Trent   I'm going as fast. As I say, first day at school. Not many people around. Shaun is not recovering at all from getting knocked out by my sister, he could barely stand up, crying like a bitch gal, begging me not to tell anyone what happened. That sister of mine could tump though, like a man, Jesus! Her and her iron fist. She'd size you up, then boosh! And I am talking about a first-class arse-whopping deluxe-combo meal, Mike Tyson style wid a side of fries – boosh, I promise you!

Gus (*losing patience*)   Trent?

Trent   Alright. Anyway, as a sign of appreciation for keeping quiet about him getting turned over by a gal, Shaun offers to take me to the *wall*, where his big brother Tommy liked to hang wid his boys, his crew. Shaun was their dogsbody, he would get their fags from the Paki shop, hold their coats, send messages, get people on the phone for them from the phone box, see that kid at the beginning of *Goodfellas*, just like him. And for all that, he would get funded. Fiver here, tenner there. Shaun told his brother, I was with him, so I would get funded as well while they worked.

Fraser   So, what did they do for work?

Trent   Everyting! Daily, nightly, cars would pull up, all kinds of trading was happening, bit of burn, pirate videos, credit cards, bottles of booze, stereos, rings, watches, name it, bruv. The best oysters and creepers from all over the manor would congregate to the *wall* most days, they'd buy, trade and feast, all night long. You'd juggle with whatever came your way. When Tommy got sent down for a ten, his crew started to scatter. Shaun and me were growing, we got to know these three (*Points to* **Gus**, **Leslie** *and* **Selwyn**.) from the children's home, soon we spent more time on the *wall* than at the home. Before we know it, this van pulls up, belonging to the Barton youth club, these boys jump out, sit on the *wall*, our *wall*, trying to move us along saying it's theirs now. Shaun weren't having it, as far as he could see, Tommy gave him that *wall* to look after till he got out. He be fucked if he was giving it up to a bunch of wannabe rugby-playing poofs! One of those Barton boys looked useful, though, really fucking. I go to Shaun, maybe we could share it, it's a long enough *wall*. Truth is, my rear end is puckering.

The guys laugh at the thought.

This Barton boy was glaring. Shaun was glaring. I'm standing in the middle of them with my arse this much away from a full evacuation. Before I know it, Shaun whips out this monkey wrench and pummels this Barton boy's face in. 'Have summa that,' he goes. No one knew what day it was, especially them

Barton boys. They just took their man and drove off, they never bothered us again. Shaun had earned his first rep, he was the talk of the manor for weeks! To this day, I have no idea where he was hiding that wrench on his person and how he whipped it out so fast. It was like it was attached to his arm or summin.

Leslie   Robo–Shaun!

Selwyn   I had both of my feet then.

Trent   That's it, Sel, bring it down for me.

Selwyn   I'm not bringing it down – fuck off, man, I'm agreeing wid yer. We was top.

Gus   I hate that word *was*, enough of it.

Selwyn   From the time.

Leslie   It was a good memory, Gus, don't spoil it, yeah?

Gus   How am I spoiling it, Les?

Leslie   You weren't even there, you were off somewhere, tapping Andrea weren't it? Or Tina, as it now appears.

Gus   I wish I was there, I should have been there. Sorted you total bell-ends out.

Leslie   Sorted out what? The Barton boys got a hiding.

Gus   It should never have got that far.

Leslie   There is no pleasing you, is there Gus? Gotta make us feel we can't do nuttin without you.

Gus   You want to ease up on the booze for me, Les?

Leslie (*to* **Trent** *and* **Selwyn**)   Why don't you two speak up for once?

Trent   You have been knocking them back, Les.

Leslie   Not me, Gus! Tell him how it go.

Gus Well come on then, Trent? Sel? Tell me how it go? What you have fer me?

Leslie They won't.

Selwyn I can speak for myself, Leslie.

Leslie So speak! Gwan nuh.

He gets a message on his phone. He reads it.

That's from Gerry, he ain't seen Shaun either. I wish Shaun was here right now. He should be here.

Gus Why? What's Shaun going to do, what's he going to say?

Leslie Go tell you about you about yourself for one thing. Give it to you straight, like always, both barrels, in yer face, right deh so!

Gus You give it to me, whatever this is, come!

Leslie (*points to* **Fraser**) Why did you not tell us about him, Gus? Sam's sister, of all the gals you could have had. Why her?

Fraser Yes, Gus, why her?

Gus Don't mek me hurt you again, younger.

Fraser I wouldn't try that.

Gus Like you have a say in any of this.

Trent Look, why don't I do a drive around again, find Shaun? (*To* **Fraser**.) Easy, puppy.

Fraser Puppy? You had an absolute mare with my boys today innit, Trent? Since I come in here, you can barely look at me.

Trent Fuck off, young one, right now. No offence, Gus.

Gus For what, he ain't nuttin to me, yer deaf?

Leslie Your *boys*, Fraser?

Fraser For real.

Leslie   But you are not *their* boy.

Gus   More like yer their bitch.

Fraser (*rages*)   What yu say!

Gus   I say bitch! B-I-T-C-H.

Fraser   Fuckin –

Gus   Don't rise up, unless yer put up!

Leslie   Hate to say, Fraser, but yer old man has a point. What were you inside for?

Fraser   Breaking and entering, assault with an offensive weapon.

Leslie   First time? Don't lie.

Fraser   Who's lying? First time, what of it?

The guys laugh.

What, what of it?

Leslie   No one ever gets caught doing summin for the first time.

Gus   Unless yer schupid!

Leslie   I can't get out of bed without groaning or feel summin inside of me is creaking, he wants to lead us out on a job. We're too old for this shit.

Fraser   You're still the firm!

Leslie   Firm of what? We got cameras everywhere now, CCTV and shit. The days of a good honest creep are gone. It's in the past, young one.

Selwyn   Why can't it be now?

Trent   Sel. Sit down.

Selwyn   Why can't it be again?

Gus (*to* **Selwyn**)   You go sit down, tek yer pills, and forget about this rhatid supermarket. (*Points to* **Fraser**.) As soon as this boy jogs on, like right fucking now. We go find Shaun, then we go do what we said we'd do, have a mighty session, drinks all round, *capice*?

Selwyn *loses it, grabs a stool and throws it across the room, then smashes some bottles along the bar.*

Gus   What the fuck is dis huh!

Selwyn   I said, why can't it be now, why can't it be again?

Gus   Lawd, help me put this fucker down!

Trent   It's alright, Gus.

Gus   I ain't alright, look what him do to my yard.

Trent   Let me handle him.

Selwyn *grabs a chair leg and begins waving it around in a frenzy.*

Selwyn   You don't speak me for me, Trent. We go do this ting, we go show everyone, who we are, Durnfield, yer understand?

Leslie   Sel?

Selwyn   No fucker go leave here till we do.

Trent   Sel, look at me, look at me, man.

Gus   Yer gonna clean this shit up.

Trent   Gus, I got this.

Selwyn   No one.

Trent   Sel! Look at me. Look at me, mate.

Selwyn *looks at him.*

Trent   Come on, bruv, you know what's next, do it for me. Do it, Sel.

Selwyn *shuts his eyes.*

Trent   This space right here, this is yours . . . This belongs to you, yeah?

Selwyn   Yeah.

Trent   Yer safe in your space, no one can trouble you in your space.

Selwyn   I won't let anyone trouble me in my space.

Trent   Is your space, yer safe, Sel, safe.

Selwyn   Safe, safe!

Trent *slowly takes the chair leg away from* **Selwyn**. *He sits him down and cradles him, almost like a child.*

Selwyn   I am safe in my space.

Trent   Yer safe. Let's do the chant. Come on. (*Ever so softly.*) *Everywhere we go.*

Selwyn   *Everywhere we go.*

Trent   *People wanna know.*

Selwyn   *People wanna know.*

Trent   *Who we are.*

Selwyn   *Who we are.*

Trent   *Shall we tell them?*

Selwyn   *Shall we tell them?*

Trent   *We know our manners.*

Selwyn   *We know our manners.*

Trent   *We fight with spanners.*

Selwyn   *We fight with spanners . . .*

Trent/Selwyn   *We are respected, wherever we go. Doors and windows open wide, open wide! We are the Durnfield boys, once again, we are the Durnfield boys!*

Trent   Peace.

Selwyn's *eyes remain closed.* **Trent** *leaves him to rest and turns round to face the others.*

Leslie   Nice.

Gus   Last time I heard that tune, we had Man U at Wembley.

Leslie   1990?

Gus (*chants*)   *Ian Wright, Wright, Wright!*

Leslie   Ninety-second minute.

Gus   The size of my erection.

Leslie   The sound of your voice. I lost all hearing in my left ear.

Trent   I bring the chant back out every now and then. Helps him remember, to relax and shit. He shouldn't drink so much. It messes up his medication.

Gus   It tek him to trash my yard for you to say that?

Trent   I'll fund you for the damage, Gus.

Gus   With what? My corn? So basically I am funding myself.

Trent   I'll find you the corn yeah? I'll graft 24/7 if I have to.

Leslie   No one grafts any more, Trent. It's over!

Trent   I ain't over.

Leslie   You are a fifty-year-old white-van man, deal wid it.

Trent   I'm forty-nine.

Leslie   Sorry, my mistake.

Trent   I had a six-pack once.

Leslie   Oh!

Trent   You remember my six-pack?

Leslie   Lawd Jesus!

Trent   Tell me I didn't look criss back then? Tell me, Les! That when it comes to getting wid gal, any gal, I could leave you all behind. Tell me I didn't lay my pipe all over South, yer cunt. Tell me, if you lie, you die. I want that shit back, brudda.

Gus   Join a rhatid gym then.

Leslie   Or come swimming with me.

Trent   Say what?

Leslie   Come swimming with me, and Jan.

Trent   I can't swim, Les.

Leslie   She can teach you.

Trent   Teach me?

Leslie   It's all about believing you're not going to drown, Trent, just float. That's what she did for me, she held me up in the pool, I just lied back in her arms, and I trusted her.

Trent   I ain't lying down in no pool for your woman, fuck off, Les.

Gus   Gym it is then. I bought one, you know. I'll let you join for a discount, Trent.

Leslie   Gus with the jokes now.

Gus   I ain't laughing, Les, I am crying. I am welling up in here, fer trut. All night, I can't believe what I have been hearing. Trent sweating bacon cos of some youts, Selwyn close to tears. You panting for the love of some uppity white bitch.

Leslie   Leave it, Gus.

Gus   You'll be baking biscuits next. We're the Durnfield boys, what de rass happened to that?

Trent (*points to* **Fraser**)   Him is what happened for a start. Maybe you should focus on straightening him out.

Gus   Damn right, I go straighten him out right now.

Enough of this fuck ries.

He grabs **Fraser** *and drags him to the door.*

Fraser   Yes, Gus, do what she said you would do.

Gus   Yes, know-it-all Tina, knows it all right?

Fraser   I didn't mean Mum.

Gus   Who then?

Fraser   Did you even ask her if she even wanted to go to that school? Did you not check her face when you told her?

Gus   Say that to me again?

Fraser   That she was happy where she was?

Gus   Naomi?

Fraser   That she doesn't want to be where you want her to be?

Gus   What the fuck you doing wid her?

Fraser   We found each other on Facebook.

Gus   I don't give a rass lick where you find her.

Fraser   She my sister.

Gus   You ain't nuttin to her. You stay away from her.

Fraser   Joke is, she is only trying to help you.

Gus   Shut yer mout.

Fraser   She heard you on the phone, dread.

Gus   Don't call me *dread*.

Fraser   To the bank.

Leslie   Oh, yes?

Fraser   Business tight, can't afford the fees.

Gus   Shut yer damn mout!

Leslie   Yer empire starting to crumble, Gus?

Gus   It ain't gonna happen.

Leslie   Sounds like it already is, mate.

Gus   Ca' I don't pussy out on tings, I see shit through.

Leslie   Unlike the rest of us, that's what you mean, right?

Trent   Lawd please, mek Shaun walk through this door right now, so we can end this foolishness.

Selwyn   Shaun?

Trent   Space, Selwyn, yer personal space.

Fraser   Why do you hate me so much?

Gus   I don't know you.

Fraser   You used to know me. Or maybe it's Mum you hate?

Gus   She don't mean nuttin to me. She still want me to say I'm sorry about Sam, you want me to say I'm sorry. I'm done wid saying sorry.

Fraser   Bwoi, she really got to you, innit?

Gus   Fraser, I'm going to give you ten seconds, yeah.

Fraser   That's the first time you said my name all night.

Gus   Five seconds.

Fraser   Fuck yer then. Fuck him! Who's wid me? Who's wid me? Come on, man, it's a sweet job, the woman will give it up, I know it.

Leslie   Like Sam did?

Fraser   Forget Sam, you lot have.

Leslie   I wish I could bwoi, believe me.

Fraser   I told you I ain't bothered by that.

Leslie   Robbing his bookies was supposed to be a sweet job. Sam was the best Oyster I ever knew, a top earner, he covered the whole of South, he would graft like no other, just don't ask

him to fight, he couldn't fight his way out of nuttin, innit boys?
So, what made him think he could tek the three of us on, I
have no idea.

Trent   Me neither.

Leslie   It was like he was in a rage about summin.

Trent   Let's move on.

Leslie   Like he knew it was us.

Trent   You done?

Leslie   It was Selwyn who hit him first. When he saw Sam
go for me. You wanna know what it's like being hit on the back
of the head by Selwyn? It's like having an anvil dropped on
yer nut. That should have been the end of it, we shoulda just
dashed right out of there, I don't know what it was, maybe we
were too coked up or summin, it was the sight of Sam trying
to get back up, like he was ready for round two. Trent started
us off, we kicked him back down, and we kept on kicking him
and kicking him, and kicking him, until it looks like his nut was
gonna explode or summin.

Fraser   Alright!

Leslie   Alright what? I thought you said you weren't bothered
by that? That's yer uncle, our friend. We are the reason why
he can't wipe his own arse any more 'bout. Alright? That does
not bother you, not even a touch? Bwoi, I have known some
proper bastards in my time, who have done some hardcore shit
that you wouldn't believe. But every single one of them had
the touch, even they. A touch of conscience that makes us all
human. You telling me you are badder than them, that you
have no touch, that you can see us stamping on yer uncle's
head and you don't want to fling yourself at us right now, wa'
wrong wid yu? Tell me about the supermarket, tell me about
this woman who will give it up for us, like that? Tell me, Fraser,
fucking tell me how high up you are in the BMC? Tell me you
want this, tell me nuh? Do what yer old man tells yu, tek yer

arse out of here and don't ever come back. Fuck off out of it, go. I said, jog on!

Fraser *leaves.*

Gus   You he listens to?

Leslie   Not bad for a mug, hey, Gus? But then we are all mugs to you, right? We all done bird, except you.

Gus   Cos I used my noodle. None of you listened, none a' yer!

Trent   So, it's our fault?

Gus   Don't even think about bringing yerself to me, Trent. Stay which part yu deh, from the time that younger come in here you bin pissing yer pants.

Trent   You would have been afraid as well, Gus.

Gus   Pussy-hole!

Trent   More scared than I have been in my life, yes, alright! Dat don't shame me.

Gus   I don't know you.

Leslie   Why did you ask him if you should say sorry?

Gus   What you on wid now?

Leslie   You asked the boy if you should say yer sorry about Sam.

Gus   Yeah, ca you idiots caved his skull in.

Leslie   Yes, us, not you.

Gus   Right?

Leslie   So why are you saying sorry?

Gus   I didn't say sorry.

Leslie   I know you didn't. But Gus, why would yer, why? It was us, not you. Why? Gus? Why? Earth calling Augustus!

Gus   Watch yourself, Leslie!

Leslie   What did you do man?

Gus   Fucking hell, Shaun. (*Calls.*) Where you at?

Selwyn   Shaun not coming.

Leslie   Sam shouldn't have been at the bookies that night. We had it planned. He wasn't supposed to be there.

Gus   Fuck is this?

Leslie   He wasn't supposed to be there, Gus. Not unless someone told him about it. Not unless he was warned.

Trent   What dis?

Leslie   Was it you, Gus? Did you warn him? Did you warn Sam, Gus? Did you tell him we were coming? Gus?

Sound of a car window being smashed outside. Car alarm goes off.

Gus   Motherfuck . . . what that?

Leslie   I'll go. Trent, keep him here.

Gus   What that? Yer gonna keep me here, Les, did I hear you right? You telling Trent to keep me here?

Leslie   Don't let him leave.

He goes outside. **Trent** *blocks* **Gus***'s path.*

Gus   Don't fuck around, Trent, not tonight.

Trent *blocks* **Gus***'s path again.*

Gus   Trent? Behave yourself now.

Trent   Come on, Gus.

Gus   'Come on, Gus'? Come on, Gus, what?

Trent   Don't do this.

Gus   You really tink you are gonna stop me? Do you want to make one with me now?

Trent   Gus?

Gus   You and yer fat arse.

Trent   Don't.

Gus   Mister Waga Waga, gonna put me down at last? Feel free to slap yourself hard for even thinking that.

Trent   Just calm down, please?

Gus (*laughs*)   You have never lifted your hand to me in all yer entire life. Don't be an eddyatt and tink you can start now.

Trent   I'm just doing what Les say.

Gus   'What Les say'? Am I a prick? Since when you start taking orders from the *white boy*?

Trent   Come on, Gus, we're not eleven no more.

Gus   Since when, Trent?

Trent   Les ain't no *white boy*.

Gus   Then what is he?

Trent   What you mean . . . he's Durnfield. He's one of the firm, he's us!

Gus   He can fuck off, him and his ho!

Trent   Oh, that is scathing.

Gus   You go move?

Trent   Ever since you went all suit and tie on us, it's like yer soul just left. I can't deal, Gus.

Gus   You go cry in front of me again?

Trent   I wasn't crying.

Gus   Pussy-ole, you dat!

Trent   You didn't tell Sam about us, did yer? Did yer?

Gus   Move.

Trent   Fer trut, Gus? Did you put him on us?

Gus   Mi say move!

Leslie *comes back inside, dragging* **Fraser** *along with him.*

Gus   Tell me it ain't what I think it is?

Leslie   I can't help you there.

Gus   My car?

Leslie   He went all medieval on it. Glass everywhere.

Gus (*looks outside*)   Oh, dis bwoi. Dis fucking bwoi!

He goes for **Fraser**. **Leslie** *blocks him.*

Gus   You as well, Les?

Leslie   Tell me first.

Gus   Mind out of my way, Les –

Leslie   Tell me about Sam first

Gus   So I can dead him right now.

Leslie   You told him, you told Sam, you told him we were coming. Didn't you? Fucking didn't you? I know it, you flapped your gums to him. You told him we were going to rob him. I know you did it.

Trent   Tell him he is talking shit, Gus. For me, man, please, tell him!

Leslie   Yes, Gus, you tell me, you tell me now. Tell me, I am talking shit. Tell them too, tell them!

Gus   So, what was I supposed to do, Leslie?

Leslie   You did?

Gus   What was I supposed to do?

Leslie   You did. Oh God.

Gus   Was I really supposed to stand by, and watch you lot fuck yourselves in the arse?

Trent   Oh, Jesus, man! This is rass!

Leslie   Fuck what, Gus? Fuck what? It was a sweet plan, sweeter still if Sam weren't there.

Gus   That give you the right to teif him?

Leslie   Fuck's sake, it's what we do.

Gus (*points to* **Fraser**)   No, it's what they do! He was one of us.

Leslie   He left us. He walked away. He wanted to be a taxpayer. That gave us the right to fleece him, like any other mark.

Gus   Shit don't mek it right.

Leslie   This coming from you who was poking Sam's little sister behind his back? Yes, you are a proper gent aren't you, Gus?! Fifteen years old.

Gus   Fuck off from me.

Leslie   We were bruc. We were grafting 24/7, but no one was trading on the *wall*, no dough was coming in. You know how it was.

Gus   So, why you nuh come to me?

Leslie   We just wanted to do something different, anything, make links of our own.

Gus   I would have funded you all, till death, you know that.

Leslie   That didn't involve you, because all you do is bark orders, tell us we can't make moves. Going on about the good old days of the firm, all of us, all on the *wall*, rubbing our faces in it with your success, wid your money. Only showing up when you are fucking rolling around in it.

Gus   Oh come outta my range if yer gonna cry about it.

Leslie   They tore down our *wall*, Gus. They bloody tore it down, and for what? To build some fucking flats that no one I know can afford? And you bought one of them.

Gus   I bought three actually.

Leslie   Oh, you fuck.

Trent   Gus man?

Gus   Shut yer noise, Trent, just for once. You think I didn't know things were on the slide for us, Les? That everyone out there had deh tings on a lock-down? I saw it coming. Why didn't you? That I didn't know you muppets were gonna do summin stupid? As soon as you started sniffing the white, I knew. And you fucked it up like I knew you would.

Leslie   You fucked it for us.

Trent   You break my heart man, Gus. See it deh!

Gus   You break mine! Wid yer rass claart tears.

Leslie   Fuck is this anyhow? What the fuck is this?

Gus   This is your family, Les. We cater for each other.

Leslie   Fuck this family. Fuck all of it, you hear me, fuck it! Jan's my family now, and she's at home waiting for me.

Gus   We wait for Shaun.

Selwyn   Shaun's not coming

Trent (*losing patience*)   Sel?

Leslie   I got a woman waiting for me, Gus. A woman who loves me, finally. She's got a nice cup of herbal tea ready for me, I bet.

Gus   You must be getting deaf in yer old age, Leslie, we wait for Shaun.

Leslie   You wait for Shaun, I'm gone.

Gus   Yer been a total pussy about this, I hope you know that.

Leslie   I'm gone, Gus, I'm done. Don't make stay.

Gus   Why?

Leslie (*snaps*)   Cos I will fucking dead you, as God is mine.

Gus   Come nuh.

Leslie (*composes himself*)   No.

Gus   Come nuh!

Leslie   She wouldn't want me to.

Gus   Oh this fucking Jan.

Leslie   Get off it, Gus.

Gus   She tamed you good.

Leslie   Don't!

Gus   You wouldn't be crying this much if she was an ebony now would yer?

Leslie   Oh what de fuck?

Gus   Would yer? Would yer?

Leslie   It's my heart that is breaking now as well, Gus.

Gus   Would yer, Les? While I'm on it, how long do you think you can keep her, you with no pot to piss in, Mister Jobseeker Allowance? How long before she gets bored, dumps like you like a cold, marries some rich white fuck, then one Easter Sunday she can brag to her herbal-tea-drinking dykes about how she went slumming for a bit of rough down South.

Leslie   Jan is good for me.

Gus   Jan's a cunt.

Leslie   She saved my life. She's God's gift.

Gus   Does she make you leave your balls at the front door, Les?

Leslie   Not working, Gus.

Gus   Does she have to show you where to put it now?

Trent   Oh over the line, mate.

Gus   I bet she does.

Leslie   Jan made me know I am better than this. That I don't want this. That I am too bloody old for it. Shaun would dead you right now, if he was here, Gus, he would dead you.

Selwyn (*getting louder*)   Shaun not coming.

Leslie   Trent, shut him up, nuh!

Trent   Shaun not coming, what you mean Sel?

Selwyn   Him not coming is what I mean.

Trent   How you know that?

Selwyn   He told me.

Trent   He told you?

Selwyn   You deaf?

Trent   When did he tell you?

Selwyn   Today. On the *wall.*

Trent   The *wall?*

Gus   The *wall* is gone, Sel.

Selwyn   Where there used to be the wall I mean! Outside the flats. Walking up and down like he did not know what day it was. I don't know what happen, but doing bird this time messed him up good.

Leslie   What has that to do wid him not coming, Sel?

Selwyn   He said that he couldn't deal with us any more, that he knows things had changed, that he can't go back inside not ever. He's done with grafting, he is done with us.

Gus   You didn't think you should have told us that before?

Selwyn   I thought he would change his mind

Gus   You thought?

Selwyn   I dared him to do it, to walk away from us, I said he couldn't. That me, him, all of us too tight to let that happen. I didn't think he would have the front, I knew he'd come, ca' we're solid, I just knew.

Gus   Do you see him here, Sel? Do you? Is he standing right here with us? For fuck's sake!

Leslie   Sel. You really should have told us.

Selwyn   I am telling you now.

Leslie   Before, man, before, oh what is the rhatid use? You last see him on the bridge you say, yes or no, Sel?

Selwyn   Yes!

Leslie   I gotta find him.

Gus   Is he alright now?

Trent   Yeah, he's all calm now.

Gus   Good, cos I want to tell him summin.

Trent   Gus, don't, man.

Gus   Tell him about himself, it's due. You know what, Sel, you really know what? Go back to yer supermarket, yeah, go back to your can of beans and pulses, yeah, cos that is all you are good for, and I ain't just saying that, cos you ain't no grafter, you never were, you never knew how to graft without one of us being there for you. Yu understand? Tell me you understand, you fucking waste of carbon, yer using up my oxygen, tell me, nuh!

Leslie   Gus!

Gus   Lay a hand on me again, Leslie, and it's you next, before God mi swear to you!

Leslie *removes his hand from* **Gus***'s arm.*

Leslie   I'm going to find my friend.

Gus   Him my friend too.

Leslie   I don't want you anywhere near.

Gus   You think you can stop me, Les?

Leslie   I'll stop yer.

Gus   Are you high?

Leslie   We're done. We're done.

Gus *faces* **Trent** *and* **Selwyn**.

Gus   What? What you have to say, what?

Trent   What time on Saturday, Les, for the swimming?

Gus   Are you fucking joking, Trent?

Leslie   Half-nine, Greenwich Pools.

Gus   This for real?

Trent   Deal me in.

Gus   Yes, Les, you deal him in. Gwan, Trent, go on, get your swimming cossie out, let the whole of South see yer wurtless fat-arse self. Well, go after him, like you always do, like you keep doing, you and Sel, nuttin but a dawg, the two a' yer in fact, I'll throw you a bone each, yeah, go! You still here, fucking go, will yer, jog the fuck on! Go.

Trent   Come, Sel.

Selwyn *slowly follows* **Trent** *and* **Leslie** *towards the door.*

Gus (*mocks*)   Shaun not coming, Shaun not coming, yer crazy mad up in the head one-footed fuck! (*Calls.*) Pussy dem! All a' yu! Nuttin but a wurtless fucking white boy, nuttin but a stupid fat bastard, yer waga-waga. A one-foot mad-up fool. You ain't no firm, Durnfield my arse, I was Durnfield born and true, true and born, I was the firm, me one! Me! All my life I have looked out for you, every single one of you.

Leslie (*points to* **Fraser**)   You want to look after somebody now, Gus, look after him!

Leslie *leaves followed by* **Trent** *and* **Selwyn**.

Gus *sees* **Fraser** *is still there*.

Gus   What do you want from me now? What? Fucking what?

Fraser   You owe me.

Gus   You can't still be giving it about joining the BMC? Did you hear nuttin of what Leslie said to you? Well? Big-time gangster! If you're so bad, where's yer blade? Where's yer tool?

Fraser *reveals a kitchen knife from his coat pocket*.

Gus (*laughs*)   Wat dat? What does that prove?

Fraser   You owe me.

Gus   Have you ever had a session, Fraser? An encounter? A right royal punch-up? Where you get so close you can smell the other guy's breath? When you can feel the bones in your fist cracking in half as it lands against the side of another brer's face? Have you ever in your life had one of those?

Fraser   You owe me.

Gus   Trent's right, that little fat bastard is actually right for once. You youngers scare us. You know why? Ca' yer selfish, ca' you don't give a shit about anyone but yourselves.

Fraser   This from the brer who fucked his friends over?

Gus   You would rather die than learn, innit? You know nuttin about creeping. You don't graft, you don't earn, you don't think, you just tek. Young, old. Rich, poor. It don't matter, does it? It's your world now, as fucked as it is. Slash and grab, innit?

Fraser   Well, come then, big man, school us.

Gus   Move.

Fraser   School me.

Gus   Go cry somewhere else.

Fraser   So, if I ain't got them, what else have I got?

Gus   Yer mum?

Fraser   She don't want to know, bitch dashed me out.

Gus   You speak that way about yer mudda?

Fraser   What about you? Boy, she really hurt you. She really did, some lickle yat in school uniform who couldn't keep her legs closed . . . .

Gus   Hey!

Fraser   How did you know who I was? When did you realise?

Gus   From the second you breezed yourself in here. I know dem eyes from anywhere.

Fraser   Is that why you never claimed me? Were you ashamed or summin? Was I a mistake?

Gus   Ask her.

Fraser   I done nuttin but ask her. All she does is lie and hold out.

Gus   Damn right she lies. Telling you I was bored wid her, and decided to step? That fucking lying bitch.

Fraser   Yer holding out as well, that must mek you a bitch as well, yeah?

Gus   Careful, bwoi.

Fraser   Just tell me why, man.

Gus *starts pouring several shots of whiskey.*

Fraser   You go tell me?

Gus   Let me see you do this again.

Fraser   You go tell me, Gus?

Gus   Man up, show we what you have.

Fraser *downs in one a shot of whiskey. Then another. Then another.*

Fraser   I can do this all day. Why you never tell them about me?

Gus   You are never going to go away, are you? Fuck up my night for me.

Fraser   Tell me why.

Gus   Lose the only family I have ever had. Ever wanted, ever cared about.

Fraser   Tell me.

Gus   Fucking you.

Fraser   Gus?

Gus   I ain't no perv.

Fraser   I never said.

Gus   It wasn't like that.

Fraser   So, how was it then?

Gus   I didn't want them to fuck it up for me. When the council tore our *wall* down to build flats, yeah, I cried.

Fraser *scoffs.*

Gus   I was welling up! It was the end of an era. What the rass we're going to do now, all that shit. Yer mudda walked by on her way to school, put her arm around me, she look like a gal, but she come like a woman. The way she smiled and shit. That was beautiful. She was beautiful, I wanted summin beautiful, who doesn't? You have a problem wid that? You have a problem, Fraser? Answer me, nuh!

Fraser   No, I don't have a problem with that.

Gus   One thing I wanted to keep to myself, one thing from their eyes and deh jokes, one ting!

Fraser   So what happen?

Gus   That's all yer getting.

Fraser   Come on, what happened?

Gus   Come near Naomi again, I'll bruc you in half.

Fraser   She's my sister.

Gus   She is nothing to you, you're staying away.

Fraser   She hates that school.

Gus   I don't care what she hates.

Fraser   The fess are bleeding you dry anyway.

Gus   That's my problem, not hers, not yours. You tell her from me, her arse is staying in that school, make sure that is the last thing you say to her, capice?

Fraser   Big man, Gus.

Gus   Believe that.

Fraser   Your boys have gone.

Gus   Last warning, bwoi.

Fraser   The *wall* has gone.

Gus   Hear me.

Fraser   This place, as good as gone. Gone, all gone.

Gus   Cos of you.

Fraser   Cos of you! Tell me what happened wid Mum.

Gus   Was this your plan all along?

Fraser   Tell me.

Gus   I bet it was.

Fraser   Tell me, man.

Gus (*snaps*)   Bitch gave me a choice, her or dem.

Fraser   That why you told Sam?

Gus   For all the good. As soon as you come outta her, shit started to change. Like she a full grown-up now, telling me she

don't love me no more, we ain't going anywhere. I mean, what
kind of bitch do that, a lying bitch is what, a no-good lying
free-it-up-for-anyone skank bitch who mek me feel I is nuttin
but a dirty old man instead of someone who would lie down in
traffic for her. Happy now?

Fraser   Happy?

Gus   Tek yer arse out.

Fraser   You dash me, ca' Mum dash you? I'm supposed to
be happy? No, you knew messing around with a fifteen-year-
old was a big no-no, that is why you couldn't tell yer brers, ca'
you knew it was wrong.

Gus   You need to step.

Fraser   You could at least man up about that.

Gus   You tink yer bright?

Fraser   Brighter than you.

Gus   Crying like a gal cos the BMC don't want you till you
prove yerself, that kind of bright? Why do you want to join a
gang for? Why is that so important to you? You can't even say,
can you?

Fraser   Yeah I can.

Gus   I'm listening.

Fraser   Ca' without a gang, you're an orphan. With a gang,
you walk in twos, you walk in threes and you walk in fours.
When your crew is the best, you're out in the sun, you're home
free home.

Gus   Are you quoting *West Side Story* to me?

Fraser   No!

Gus   Yeah you are, that is from *West Side Story*.

Fraser (*lying*)   No it ain't.

Gus   It is from *West Side* motherfucking *Story*! It's at the beginning of the film, Riff is with Tony asking him to join him at the dance to help take on the Sharks. You don't feel shame?

Fraser   Me shame? Well how do you know it's from that?

Gus   How you think?

Fraser (*realises*)   Yeah. I swear, Mum used to watch that film on DVD every blasted week.

Gus (*agrees*)   Who do you think bought her the DVD?

Fraser   Best part of the film for me when the guy says that. You walk in twos, threes, fours. When your crew is the best . . . It's how I feel.

Gus   But you are not part of their crew.

Fraser   It's still how I feel; you have a problem with that?

Gus   No, I don't have a problem with that.

Fraser   Cos you can jog on if you don't like it.

Gus   I got no more time for you, I got this place to open tomorrow night.

Fraser   You fucked it all up for yerself, Gus.

Gus   If by that you mean I used my head, that I made money, proper money, more corn than those fools and the whole of South put together, yeah, Fraser, I fucked it right up. I would have given her everyting but that still weren't enough for the bitch.

Fraser   You can't mek someone love you.

Gus   And you can't mek me claim you.

Fraser   She went off you, she dashed you, man up about it.

Gus   Then hold you in my arms as my own? I claim you for all of the world to see? I bet you can see it, right now you are seeing pictures. Innit? You and me, with my arm over you? Father and son! Never heard such stupidness in my life. You think I going to forget what you done to my car? You know

how much corn I shelled out for that? Let this be the last time
I tell you this. You got ten seconds to step, and I mean ten
seconds. You here a second longer, and you are cleaning this
shit up, all a' it.

Fraser Why wait?

He starts picking up pieces of glass on the floor.

Gus Lawd Jesus, wat dis bwoi doing now? What you doing?

Fraser Cleaning this shit up, you have a problem with that?

Gus You want cut yourself? All that glass, think it through
nuh, bwoi? There's a dustpan and brush behind the bar.

Fraser *finds the dustpan and brush from behind the bar. He begins
sweeping.*

Gus *picks up and tries reassembling the broken chairs and stools. After
a brief moment of silence* **Gus** *looks over at* **Fraser**.

Fraser What?

Gus A supermarket?

Fraser It got me here with you, didn't it?

Gus So you did plan all this.

Fraser She still woulda given up it, though, telling you. And
you ain't got nothing for me on that, not after what you did to
Sam.

Gus What they did to Sam.

Fraser You sent him there. Your own friend!

Gus You tink I'm proud of how it went down?

Fraser I don't give a fuck how you feel, Gus.

Gus Yet here you are.

Fraser Yep. Right here, so.

They continue to clear up in silence.

Gus When you done in here, deal wid the shit outside.

Fraser   What shit?

Gus   My car! All eighty grand of it.

Fraser   Right.

Gus   Better believe, right!

Fraser   Do summin for me.

Gus   Bwoi, I don't owe you nuttin.

Fraser   I didn't say you owe me.

Gus   You did before.

Fraser   Well, now I am asking, I am asking you to do summin for me.

Gus   What?

Fraser   Gimme a tale.

Gus   Say?

Fraser   A tale.

Gus   Just clean up this shit then fuck off out of my life.

Fraser   There must be one

Gus   There are hundreds.

Fraser   So, pick one out for me.

Gus   I tell yer, it's like you were put on this earth just to budda me.

Fraser   One tale, Gus, one tale. It go kill you? Just one? For me?

Gus   I'm in Knightsbridge one night, doing a bit of creeping at some top rich house there. I see some people coming out of it, they look like total millionaires, it was all him in his black tie, all her in her ball gown that hug de body, showing a lot of leg for herself as well. So, I wait until they speed off in their Rolls, get around the back, creep in the house, fucking workmen

in the house, doing overtime or summin, I play it cool, like I'm
working there as well, creep my way around them, easy.
I search the whole drum from top to bottom, I can't find
nothing. So it's a waste of time, it happens, I come back out of
the house, I'm on my way up to Oxford Street, I'd thought I'd
do a bit of dipping and kiting, but something was nibbling
away at me, I got as far as Kensington, I just knew, and I felt I
missed something at that house, so I goes back, I creep in
again, slid upstairs, and under the bed, just under the bed, I
find this plastic bag, and inside was this, well it just looked a
cheap little purse, I thought bullshit, but I decided to come
outside with it anyway, as I'm out, I'm looking inside, and it's
got loads of little compartments inside of it, layers, and inside
these layers I found untold designer jewellery, we are talking
Bulgari, Cartier, Chopard, De Beers, diamond rings, gold
chains, I had to be carrying at least a hundred thou worth of
gear, nice bit of tong, merry Christmas. It was on my mind to
take the stuff to the *wall*, get them sold ASAP. But I couldn't
help myself, I had to see how they looked, how it felt to be a
rich. I got home, put on my white suit I wore for Mickey's
wedding, I got the bling on, and I don't mind saying so, I
looked niiiice! Final test, I took myself into town, walked in
and out of all of the crowds going into the second half of one
of those shows, trying my luck. No one stopped me, I must
have looked well criss to them. Money talks, right? This kid
goes and lets me in, just assumed I had a ticket, I had a
blinding seat watching the last act of *Miss* fucking *Saigon*! I go,
why stop there. One of the boys had to see it, they wouldn't
believe otherwise. I had to pose, it had to be done, so I called
up Shaun, he was still South, but I goes he had to pick me up,
so up he shows, I get in the motor, and right there he was, not
only wearing the same white suit, fucking jewellery, fucking
rings, watch, necklace, everything, carbon fucking copy, but
bigger, so much bigger, and flashier, I goes where in the name
of Lawd Jesus fuck did you get all that, Shaun comes out with,
'I bought them all off a crackhead for a score.'

He roars with laughter. **Fraser** *is moved but does not show it.*

Gus   Well, you had to be there.

Fraser   Tek yer word on it.

Gus   You wanted a tale, I gave you a tale. Jog on if you don't like.

Fraser   You ain't all that.

Gus   Bored now.

Fraser   None of yer. I should have went for Les, when he told me to, I'll show him I have bloody truth.

Gus   You already did

Fraser   What you say?

Gus   By not going for him you already did show you had truth. More truth than the rest of us could ever put together, you understand? You didn't go low by not going for him, you went high, if you are half as smart as you think you are, you'd understand what that means. Don't be like me. Don't be like us, or anything like yer so-called brers. For fuck's sake just be you, yeah? That is all you've got. That is all I have for yer, young one, now you go sort my car out or what?

Fraser (*sincere*)   Dad . . .

Gus   . . . My car, gwan.

Fraser *leaves.*

Gus *gives up trying to repair the stools. He paces around the room.*

He is lost in so many thoughts and feelings.

He eyes the jukebox. He knows what to do with himself now. He turns it on. It plays 'Glad All Over'. He continues to be lost in his thoughts but manages to mouth some of the words somewhat sadly as he returns to repairing the stools.

Blackout.

For a complete listing of Bloomsbury
Methuen Drama titles, visit:

www.bloomsbury.com/drama

Follow us on Twitter and keep up to date
with our news and publications

@MethuenDrama